Mathematical Problem Solving With Deductive Reasoning

Marilynn L. Rapp Buxton

 Routledge
Taylor & Francis Group

NEW YORK AND LONDON

First published in 2007 by Prufrock Press Inc.

Published in 2021 by Routledge
605 Third Avenue, New York, NY 10017
2 Park Square, Milton Park, Abingdon, Oxon OX14 4RN

Routledge is an imprint of the Taylor & Francis Group, an informa business

Copyright © 2007 Taylor & Francis Group

Illustrated by Mike Eustis
Production Design by Marjorie Parker

ISBN: 9781593632199 (pbk)

DOI: 10.4324/9781003236498

Contents

Challenging Puzzles

Teacher's Guide

College professors and business professionals have told me, "Teach kids to work hard and how to think." I teach elementary gifted and talented students, as well as other classes, creative thinking (fluency, flexibility, originality, elaboration, and problem solving) and critical thinking (labeling, observation, analogies, classification, webbing, comparison, patterning, sequencing, syllogisms, cause and effect, table logic, and matrix logic). Most students enjoy matrix puzzles enough to ask for more!

But, how can a teacher justify "puzzle time" when there are standards to meet and no child to leave behind? What about students who finish assignments (especially math) and ask, "What should I do now?" What if you had a math matrix book?

This book is unique in that it contains challenging vocabulary and requires students to use logical reasoning and perform a variety of operations and skills that align with state and national standards (fractions, decimals, exponents, place value, sequencing, patterning, algebra, time, probability, percent, measurement, number line, ratios, area, volume, weight, and temperature). Students will make hypotheses, draw conclusions, organize information, and use syllogistic thinking. Teachers can feel confident they are providing rigor and reinforcing required skills in a format that students enjoy.

My students helped ensure that this book is kid friendly. The Table of Contents ranks puzzles from easy to challenging.

Students should be able to work independently if they heed instructions and refer to solutions for step-by-step explanation of reasoning. Teachers and parents may use solutions as an answer key or to allow students to self-check and clarify their work. Giving students the sample problem and information for working matrix puzzles (see pp. 6–8) is a good way to refresh students' memories of how logic puzzles work or to introduce the beginning matrix solver to the steps he or she should take to finish the problem.

This book may be used for alternate work during compacting, enrichment, centers, or just for fun. Students may work alone, with a partner, in a group, or whatever suits the needs of teachers and students. A student who fully understands the reasoning of a particular puzzle could demonstrate it to the class.

I hope this book will be a helpful resource for teachers who strive to provide challenging and applicable math enrichment that is enjoyable for students who love to think!

—Marilynn

How to Do Matrix Puzzles

Matrix puzzles are fun, and they are good exercise for your brain. They help you develop good critical and logical thinking skills. In this book, you have the extra challenge of performing a math operation or calculation during each puzzle.

Always read the puzzle introductions. They explain the situation and contain essential information. For example, a clue might say, "Chris likes hamburgers, and all the girls like pizza." Is Chris a girl or boy? The introduction said: "Two brothers (Chris and Eric) have a sister named Kylene." Add that with the clue and deduce that Chris is a boy, so he doesn't eat pizza. You would not be able to solve the puzzle without that information.

After you read the introduction, begin reading clues. If you discover a "no" clue, mark an X in the box where two items meet. Sometimes you can mark several boxes. For example, "A girl likes peanut butter." Mark X for all boys, but you don't know which girl likes it, so leave the girl boxes blank. If you discover a "yes" clue, mark O in the box. When you mark O, also mark X in the boxes above, beneath, and beside the O.

After you have read all of the clues and marked the boxes, look up and down and across to see if any columns or rows have only one box left. That will be a "yes" or O. There should be one O in every column and every row of a section. Try the sample below and read the solution.

Sample Matrix Puzzle

Four friends went shopping for school supplies. Each student purchased two different items, and nobody bought the same number of items. Read the clues and discover how many items each student bought.

	1	2	3	4	5	6	7	8
Claude								
Harry								
Nan								
Tom								
5				
6				
7				
8				

Clues:
1. Neither Tom nor the student who got five highlighters chose four erasers.
2. Neither Claude nor the student who purchased two notebooks bought six folders.
3. Neither Nan nor the student who bought eight markers selected three packages of paper or four erasers.
4. Neither Tom nor the student who got two notebooks purchased five highlighters or seven pencils.

Solution:

- Clue 1 tells us that Tom isn't 5 or 4, and 5 doesn't go with 4. Mark an X at the intersection of Tom and 4, Tom and 5, and 4 and 5.

- Clue 2 tells us that Claude isn't 2 or 6, and 2 doesn't go with 6. Mark an X at the intersection of Claude and 2, Claude and 6, and 2 and 6.

- Clue 3 tells us that Nan isn't 8, 3, or 4, and 8 doesn't go with 3 or 4. Mark an X at the intersection of Nan and 8, Nan and 3, Nan and 4, 8 and 3, and 8 and 4.

- Clue 4 tells us that Tom isn't 2, 5, or 7, and 2 doesn't go with 5 or 7. Mark an X at the intersection of Tom and 2 (Tom and 5 is already marked X from Clue 1), Tom and 7, 2 and 5, and 2 and 7. So, 2 goes with 8 (only one left). Mark an O at the intersection of 2 and 8 and an X at the intersection of 1 and 8.

Answers: After further deduction, you find that Claude is 4 and 7, Harry is 2 and 8, Nan is 1 and 5, and Tom is 3 and 6.

Hints for Solving Matrix Puzzles

Some puzzles contain three or more sections such as first name, last name, and someone's favorite hobby. Be careful to mark only one section of the matrix. Sometimes you know first and last name, first name and hobby, or last name and hobby. Transfer information from one section to another using syllogistic thinking. A syllogism says, "Apples are fruit. Fruit is good to eat. Therefore, apples are good to eat." Use syllogistic thinking on this clue:

Anne likes purple. The girl who likes purple sings well. Therefore, _____ sings well.

You would mark Anne with purple, purple with sings well, and Anne with sings well.

Carefully read clues to get correct and complete information. Here are a few other examples:

1. If a clue says, "Neither Tara nor the banker drove a car," that means three things: Tara didn't drive a car, the banker didn't drive a car, and Tara is not the banker.

2. A clue such as "The three girls are Mindy, the one wearing the red sweater, and the one whose birthday is in July" indicates three different people. Mindy doesn't wear the red sweater and her birthday is not in July. The one wearing a red sweater does not have a birthday in July.

3. Combine information from clues. Look for the same topic in several clues. Clue 1 says, "Lynn's last name is Brown." Clue 3 says, "Mrs. Brown rides a motorcycle." Clue 5 says, "Lynn is a teacher." Combine the clues about Lynn and Brown to find that Lynn Brown is a teacher who rides a motorcycle.

Solutions for Matrix Puzzles

Solutions for each of the puzzles can be found in the back of the book. Use the descriptions to help you if you get stuck on a puzzle. Your teacher may use the solutions to check your accuracy or you may self-check your own answers.

You're "Bus"ted!

Six friends are in the same class at school, but they all live in different neighborhoods. They each ride a different bus (#4, #5, #8, #10, #12, or #15) to middle school. Read the clues and determine the correct bus number for each student.

Clues

1. Shaman's bus number is ½ of Ryeisha's bus number.
2. Winston's bus number is two times Ellsworth's bus number.
3. Ellsworth's bus number is ⅓ of Gina's bus number.
4. Ami's bus number is three times Shaman's bus number.
5. Ryeisha rides a bus that has a lower number than Winston's.

	Bus #4	Bus #5	Bus #8	Bus #10	Bus #12	Bus #15
Ami						
Ellsworth						
Gina						
Ryeisha						
Shaman						
Winston						

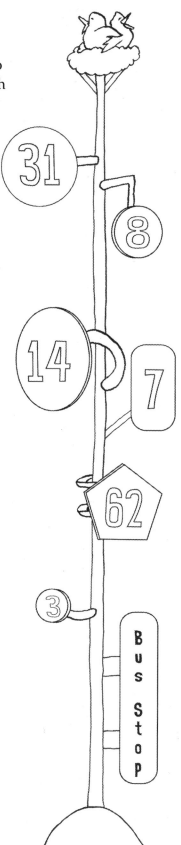

Math Logic Mysteries © Taylor & Francis Group

Card Sharks

Five neighbors (two boys named Lukas and Walker, and three girls named Elizabeth, Hannah, and Michelle) play together nearly every afternoon during school breaks. They especially enjoy strategy card games. On one particular day, they played several rousing games of Blitz-O. Each tried to avoid being the first to earn more than 100 points. However, some tried to amass exactly 100 points in order to "blitz" the other players and win the game. Use your knowledge of decimals to determine the correct score for each player. For example, .5 (half) of 90 equals 45.

Clues
1. One player had 27 points less than one of her opponents.
2. Lukas was trying to make an even 100 points so he could blitz his opponents, but he didn't quite make it. His score was .9 of Elizabeth's.
3. Walker had one disastrous round when he scored 12 of the 13 possible points. He ended up with .7 of Elizabeth's score.
4. Hannah often avoided gathering too many points. Her final score was .5 of Michelle's.

	54	63	81	90	108
Elizabeth					
Hannah					
Lukas					
Michelle					
Walker					

Math Logic Mysteries © Taylor & Francis Group   DOI: 10.4324/9781003236498-3

Frac Attack

Yesterday, seven students played a math game at school called "Frac Attack." In one particular round of the game, each student drew a card that contained one of these fractions: ⅗, ⅝, ⁷⁄₁₁, ⁸⁄₁₃, ¹³⁄₂₁, ¹⁴⁄₂₃, and ¹⁷⁄₂₈. To play, everyone simultaneously lays their card face up on the table and observes the numbers on the cards. Players have 15 seconds to claim aloud that they believe their fraction is the smallest or largest number. Titan stated he believed had the smallest number and Danette proposed she had the largest number. To calculate the missing decimals, divide the numerator by the denominator. Round the numbers to the nearest thousandths place, and write the answers in the grid. Then, read the clues to determine what fraction was on each student's card. Were Titan and Danette's claims correct?

Clues

1. Anya's number was less than .625 and greater than .607.
2. The decimal equivalent for Titan's card was not .607. For Danette's card, it was not .619. Neither one's fraction equaled .615.
3. Guy's fraction was less than Danette's but greater than Chachi's and Titan's.
4. Anya had neither ¹⁴⁄₂₃, nor the decimal equivalent .619, and Guy had neither ⅝, nor the decimal equivalent .609.
5. Chachi's number was less than Titan's. Jaquirius' fraction equaled 60%.
6. Danette's number was greater than Guy's and less than Evonne's equivalent.

Decimals ➤							
Fractions ➤	⅗	¹⁷⁄₂₈	¹⁴⁄₂₃	⁸⁄₁₃	¹³⁄₂₁	⅝	⁷⁄₁₁
Anya							
Chachi							
Danette							
Evonne							
Guy							
Jaquirius							
Titan							

Math Logic Mysteries © Taylor & Francis Group

I Am Just a Rec

For their assignment in Trie Angle's geometry class, students were asked to estimate and then calculate the area of a rectangular glass window that measured 4 ⅗ feet by 6 ⅞ feet. Students knew that to find the area, they would multiply length times width. Mr. Angle offered a holographic pencil to the student whose estimate was closest to the correct answer. Students then calculated the area and discovered whose guess was most accurate. Solve the matrix to find out which student estimated each answer, and then use the above dimensions to calculate who guessed closest.

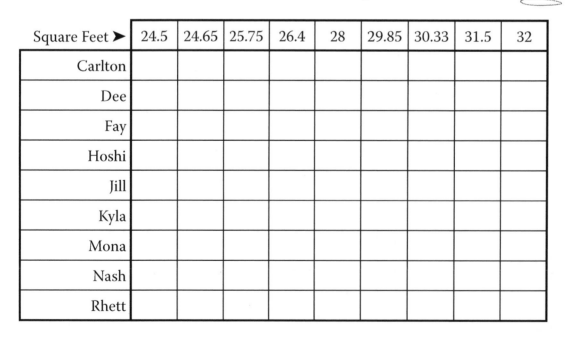

Clues

1. Neither Hoshi nor Rhett guessed 24.65, 30.33, 31.5, or 32 sq. ft.
2. Kyla and Rhett thought the area would be 25.75, 26.4, 28, or 32 sq. ft.
3. Neither Carlton, Fay, Jill, nor Rhett estimated 24.5, 28, 30.33, or 32 sq. ft. as the area.
4. Fay guessed 24.65, 26.4, or 29.85 sq. ft., and Mona estimated 24.5, 28, or 30.33 sq. ft.
5. Carlton, Dee, Mona, and Rhett guessed 24.5, 26.4, 29.85, and 31.5 square feet.
6. Dee thought the area was about 26.4 or 31.5 sq. ft., and Carlton's best estimate was 26.4 or 29.85 sq. ft.

Square Feet ➤	24.5	24.65	25.75	26.4	28	29.85	30.33	31.5	32
Carlton									
Dee									
Fay									
Hoshi									
Jill									
Kyla									
Mona									
Nash									
Rhett									

 Math Logic Mysteries © Taylor & Francis Group DOI: 10.4324/9781003236498-5

This Arm Has Charm

Six members of a summer league decided to have a friendly softball throw competition. Three boys and three girls went to the diamond. Each one lined up at home plate, wound up, and heaved the ball as far as possible. Each player recorded his or her best throw out of five. Calculate the percentages stated in the clues. For example, say a player threw 10% farther than 90 feet. Then, 10% of 90 (.1 × 90) is 9 feet more than 90, or 99 feet. If someone threw 40% less than 120 feet, he or she threw 48 feet less, or 72 feet. Match each player with the best distance he or she threw.

Clues

1. Hallie threw the softball 50% as far as Chaisa.
2. Denzel tossed the ball 100% farther than Kirah.
3. Yuri's best throw was 75% as far as Norman's best toss.
4. Norman launched the ball 50% farther than Hallie did.

	65 ft.	80 ft.	90 ft.	120 ft.	130 ft.	160 ft.
Chaisa						
Denzel						
Hallie						
Kirah						
Norman						
Yuri						

DOI: 10.4324/9781003236498-6

Need for Speed

Eight friends were competing in their town's annual go-cart races. Individuals create unique motorized go-carts and race for prize money and prestige. Each of these friends enlisted help from a teacher to construct their vehicle. Each individual drove three races and used the fastest time of the three as his or her official clocking. Can you determine how many miles per hour each driver reached in his or her go-cart?

Clues

1. Daniel's go-cart went 2 mph slower than Ryan's and 2 mph faster than Angela's.
2. Allison clocked 2 mph faster than Kelly and 2 mph slower than Nina.
3. Neither Daniel's nor Kelly's best times were faster than Rachel's.
4. Angela's go-cart went half as fast as Ryan's go-cart.

	4 mph	5 mph	6 mph	8 mph	10 mph	12 mph	14 mph	15 mph
Allison								
Angela								
Daniel								
Kelly								
Megan								
Nina								
Rachel								
Ryan								

 Math Logic Mysteries © Taylor & Francis Group   DOI: 10.4324/9781003236498-7

Let's Party!

Six friends planned a surprise birthday barbecue for Jess Jenkins and 40 other friends. The girls (Bekkah, Cassidy, and Mareesa) designed and sent the invitations. Each of the six kids contributed food or other items, including hamburger meat, buns, baked beans, potato chips, sodas, condiments, utensils, and paper products. Everyone spent a different amount of money on different items. Calculate the amounts spent and deduce which friend donated which items. What was the total amount of money spent on the party?

Clues

1. Costs included: 48 cans of soda at 33 cents per can; 8 cans of beans at $2.19 per can; 4 bags of chips at $2.69 per bag; 12 lbs of hamburger meat at $1.89 per pound; 4 dozen buns at $1.59 per dozen (plus ketchup costing $1.83, mustard costing $.94, and pickles costing $5.12); and paper items (napkins at $2.64, 3 pkgs. of paper plates at $1.24 each, 3 boxes of plastic ware at $1.44 each, and decorations for $6.98).
2. Mareesa spent more money than Jordon, but less than Victor. Cassidy spent less than Bekkah, but more than Leonard.
3. Neither Bekkah nor Leonard bought sodas and neither Jordon nor Victor bought beans.
4. A boy bought the meat to grill and Cassidy did not purchase paper products.
5. Leonard spent more than the one who bought chips and less than the girl who bought sodas. Mareesa bought chips or sodas.

Costs ➤	$	$	$	$	$	$
	chips	hamburger buns and condiments	sodas	beans	decorations, paper items, plastic ware	hamburger meat
Bekkah						
Cassidy						
Jordon						
Leonard						
Mareesa						
Victor						

Game Girl

Amber, Anna Maria, Chadron, and Macalester are good friends. They are quite unique young women in that each girl's first name is the same as the college or university that her mother attended, and each girl's last name is the same as the college or university that her father attended. One afternoon, they trekked to the arcade at the shopping mall for a little scoochball competition. Each girl earned a different number of points during her game. Read the clues to figure out each girl's first and last name and her score.

Clues

1. Anna Maria's last name is not Drexel.
2. Macalester scored more points than Anna Maria, but less than Miss Grinnell.
3. Miss Bradley scored half as many points as Amber.
4. Miss Drexel scored twice as many points as Miss Marshall.
5. Macalester scored half as many points as Miss Grinnell.

	Bradley	Drexel	Grinnell	Marshall	1,550	2,250	3,100	4,500
Amber								
Anna Maria								
Chadron								
Macalester								
1550								
2250								
3100								
4500								

Math Logic Mysteries © Taylor & Francis Group   DOI: 10.4324/9781003236498-9

Model Behavior

The city of Westwood needed a brochure to showcase various activities the city has to offer. Five children (two girls named Aleene and Kristen, and three boys named Cooper, Roberto, and Sebastian) were selected to model in places of interest to children. Each child was photographed by a professional publicist in a different location on a different day of the week. Read the clues and determine the location and day each child was photographed.

Clues

1. Roberto's photo shoot was the day before Aleene's and the day after a boy's photo was taken at the restaurant.
2. A girl was photographed at the zoo 2 days after one child posed at the airport and one day before Sebastian's photo shoot.
3. The session at the mall was later in the week than the one at the ice cream shop.
4. Photographs of Aleene, the child at the zoo, and Sebastian were taken on three successive days.

	airport	ice cream shop	mall	restaurant	zoo	Monday	Tuesday	Wednesday	Thursday	Friday
Aleene										
Cooper										
Kristen										
Roberto										
Sebastian										
Monday					
Tuesday					
Wednesday					
Thursday					
Friday					

Roundabout

Math teacher Ima Vowel has decided her parents had a wonderful sense of humor in naming her. She enjoys playing up her "Vowel" name by giving the students whose names start with vowels a special problem to work each Monday morning. The last problem required students to round numbers to the nearest thousand. Read the clues to find out which problem each student solved. Then, identify which students correctly rounded their numbers and what mistakes others made.

Clues

1. Indigo's number was larger than Ebony's but smaller than Alvin's.
2. Iva Jane's number was larger than 60,000, but Osborn's was smaller than 60,000.
3. Olathe and Ebony rounded 5-digit numbers, while Ewing and Uma rounded either 4-digit or 6-digit numbers.
4. Osborn's number was smaller than Ebony's, but larger than Ewing's.
5. Alvin and Indigo did not round 17,681 or 74,032, but rounded the numbers in between those two.
6. Uma's number was larger than Ewing's, but smaller than Iva Jane's.

Original Number ➤	4,559	5,858	17,681	30,499	63,812	74,032	146,913	728,196
Your Answers ➤								
Students' Answers ➤	4,560	6,000	18,700	30,500	64,000	74,000	150,000	728,000
Alvin								
Ebony								
Ewing								
Indigo								
Iva Jane								
Olathe								
Osborn								
Uma								

Math Logic Mysteries © Taylor & Francis Group   DOI: 10.4324/9781003236498-12

20 Questions

Students at Quest Elementary formed an afterschool math club. One day they learned about the number line. Negative numbers are left of zero (less than 0) and positive numbers are right of zero (more than 0). In a game called "20 Questions," a teacher randomly assigned eight students a number between -10 and +10. Club member Milroy Buchanan was the "inquisitor." He could pose up to 20 questions of the students in order to deduce their numbers. He used his knowledge of the number line and correctly paired each number with each student. Read the clues below and see if you can also determine the number each student was assigned. *Note:* NL stands for number line.

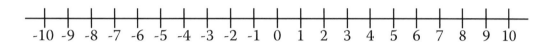

-10 -9 -8 -7 -6 -5 -4 -3 -2 -1 0 1 2 3 4 5 6 7 8 9 10

Clues

1. Milroy guessed 10 for Juan. "No. Go left on the NL. I am 8 less than Olivia," Juan replied.
2. Milroy asked Trent if he had -7. Trent said to go right on the NL to a positive single digit.
3. Milroy guessed -4 for Effie. She said, "Nope! Go right on the NL. My number is a cube."
4. "Barclay, do you have 1?" inquired Milroy. Barclay replied, "No. Go left on the NL. My number is 18 less than Trent's number."
5. "Hunan, do you have 1?" asked Milroy. "Go left on the NL." Hunan said, "My number times 3 equals -12."
6. Milroy asked, "Kelci, would I add 13 to your number to get Merrick's?" She nodded yes.

	-9	-7	-4	-3	1	8	9	10
Barclay								
Effie								
Hunan								
Juan								
Kelci								
Merrick								
Olivia								
Trent								

DOI: 10.4324/9781003236498-13

Cash for Camp

Jaleesa needed $200 to pay her tuition to camp. She asked her neighbors if they would hire her to help with chores around their houses. Each neighbor agreed to have her come twice to help with different tasks, including dusting furniture, washing and folding the laundry, mowing the grass, painting bedrooms, and pulling weeds in the garden. Jaleesa earned the following total amounts for her tasks: $20, $30, $40, $50, and $60. Can you figure out which task Jaleesa did for each neighbor and how much she was paid for doing it?

Clues

1. The five neighbors are the ones who paid $15 per task, Esther, the one who asked Jaleesa to mow the grass, Jacque, and the one who paid $30 per task.
2. Linda and the one who had Jaleesa do laundry paid $20 and $10 per task.
3. The five neighbors are the one who paid $25 per task, Chondra, the one who had Jaleesa paint, the one who paid $20 per task, and Jacque.
4. The woman who had Jaleesa dust furniture did not pay $25 or $30 per task.

	dusting	laundry	mowing	painting	weeding	$20	$30	$40	$50	$60
Chondra										
Esther										
Helene										
Jacque										
Linda										
$20					
$30					
$40					
$50					
$60					

Math Logic Mysteries © Taylor & Francis Group   DOI: 10.4324/9781003236498-14

It's Off to Work We Go

The dads of five friends work long hours each day to provide for their families. Last Friday, each child asked his or her father to write down the time he left for work and the time he arrived back at home. Each dad spent a different length of time traveling and working, and each father has a different occupation. Use the times logged by the fathers to calculate how long they were gone from home. Use the clues to match each child with his or her dad's work hours and job.

Clues

1. Devin's dad spent the least time at work. He is not the nurse.
2. The gardener was gone 9 hours, 32 minutes.
3. The dentist worked 8 hours, 45 minutes. He is not Marley's dad.
4. The janitor is Jacy's dad. He was gone 11 minutes longer than Georgia's dad.

	8:32 a.m.–5:17 p.m.	10:24 p.m.–7:43 a.m.	7:51 a.m.–4:18 p.m.	3:16 p.m.–12:59 a.m.	6:39 a.m.–4:11 p.m.	carpenter	dentist	gardener	janitor	nurse
Devin										
Elaine										
Georgia										
Jacy										
Marley										
carpenter										
dentist										
gardener										
janitor										
nurse										

Math Logic Mysteries © Taylor & Francis Group

The Quad Squad

On April 4, 1984 (04-04-84), four identical girls were born to Ford and Fortina Forley at 4 a.m. Growing up, the Forley quadruplets were very close and did nearly everything together. After high school the four sisters all decided to take law enforcement training. The city of Fourton hired them all as officers, which can be confounding to the public! Last Fourth of July, each woman arrested someone for using illegal fireworks on Independence Day. Each arrest was made at a different time (all containing 2 fours, of course) and at a different address (fours again!). Can you determine where and when each officer made her arrest?

Clues

1. Kyra made her arrest 14 hours and 4 minutes after the arrest on Monty Road.
2. Sabrina made an arrest 11 hours and 20 minutes after the one on Lindner Terrace.
3. Debra arrested a man 2 hours and 10 minutes after Helena made her arrest.
4. The house number where the arrest was made at 4:48 p.m. was lower than the house number on North 24th St.

	3449 Hunter Avenue	4046 Lindner Terrace	4418 Monty Road	4774 North 24th St	2:44 a.m.	4:54 a.m.	4:14 p.m.	4:48 p.m.
Debra								
Helena								
Kyra								
Sabrina								
2:44 a.m.								
4:54 a.m.								
4:14 p.m.								
4:48 p.m.								

Math Logic Mysteries © Taylor & Francis Group DOI: 10.4324/9781003236498-16

He's Far, Far Away

Members of the Midesta Wilderness Boys Club have an annual Racecar Derby. Boys create a vehicle that will, hopefully, roll the farthest on the derby track. One requirement is that ¾ of each vehicle must contain materials gathered from the nearby woods. At the contest each boy releases his vehicle down a steep 8-ft. incline, and the distance is measured from the bottom of the ramp to the back end of the car where it stops completely. At this year's derby, six boys made the 40-ft. distance finals. Can you use the clues to determine how far each finalist's car traveled?

Clues

1. Jack's car rolled ⅘ as far as Mitchell's car.
2. Denton's car went ¾ the distance that of Alabaster's car.
3. Perry's car cruised ⅛ farther than Jack's car.
4. Garrett's car rolled 3 feet less than Perry's car and 3 feet farther than Jack's car.

	42 ft.	48 ft.	51 ft.	54 ft.	56 ft.	60 ft.
Alabaster						
Denton						
Garrett						
Jack						
Mitchell						
Perry						

DOI: 10.4324/9781003236498-17

The Octagon

Eight friends live together in a college dormitory known as "The Oc," because of its eight-sided shape. The entrance, bathrooms, showers, weight room, and study rooms are on the lower level. A circular stairway leads to the center of the upper level where the large living room, dining area, and kitchen are located. Bedrooms are on each of eight corners. Each bedroom has a window, but the one on the south corner gets the most sunlight. Use the clues to figure out which student has which bedroom. Remember that a circle has 360°, so 180° is straight across, 90° is a right angle corner, and 45° is half of a right angle, so each room is located right next to another room.

Clues

1. Jackson's room is 180° from Vince's, and Efrem's is 180° from Orvil's.
2. Curtis' room is 90° from Vince's, and Arvin's is 90° from Orvil's room.
3. Hakeem's is 45° from Vince's, and Clint's is 45° from Arvin's.
4. Clint loves getting the most sunlight.
5. Jackson gets the hottest afternoon sun, and Efrem gets a lot of morning light.
6. Hakeem is 180° from Arvin.

	N	NE	E	SE	S	SW	W	NW
Arvin								
Curtis								
Efrem								
Hakeem								
Jackson								
Clint								
Orvil								
Vince								

Math Logic Mysteries © Taylor & Francis Group   DOI: 10.4324/9781003236498-18

Math Match

Mr. Willis offers Friday math challenges to his students. He assigns four students two problems each. Whoever correctly answers both problems first is "Math Champ" for the week. Last week's problems dealt with converting weights and measures. He said 1 kilometer (km) = ⅝ of a mile and 1 kilogram (kg) = 2.2046 pounds. Calculate the conversions for each problem and write your answers in the matrix. Write km as mixed fractions in miles and kg as decimals (round to nearest thousandths) in pounds. Compare your answers to the students' answers. Read the clues to determine which two conversion problems each student solved. Who had both answers correct and who was named "Math Champ" last Friday?

Clues

1. Pierson did not answer 4 ⅜ miles, 11.023 pounds, or 15.423 pounds. The student who answered 8.819 pounds did not figure 4 ⅜ miles.
2. Libby did not answer 3 ¼ miles or do the 4 km or 9 km problems, and Akira did not answer 2 ½ or 3 ¼ miles, but he thought 4 kg equaled 8.819 lbs.
3. Kesia did not answer 11.023 pounds, and Pierson did not answer 2 ½ miles.

	miles	miles	miles	miles	pounds	pounds	pounds	pounds
Your Answers ➤ **Students' Answers ➤**	2 ½ miles	3 ¼ miles	4 ⅜ miles	5 ⅖ miles	8.819 pounds	11.023 pounds	15.423 pounds	19.841 pounds
Problems ➤	4 km	5 km	7 km	9 km	4 kg	5 kg	7 kg	9 kg
Akira								
Kesia								
Libby								
Pierson								
4 kg or 8.819 lbs								
5 kg or 11.023 lbs								
7 kg or 15.423 lbs								
9 kg or 19.841 lbs								

Clean as a Whistle

Mrs. Dillan took her four children shopping last Wednesday. The kids plucked products off the shelves and put them in the cart. After returning home, their mother made putting away the groceries into a math game. She read how many fluid ounces were in four different cleaning products. She told the children that 16 fluid ounces = 473.176473 mL. Each child calculated the number of milliliters (mL) of one product before he or she put it away in a cupboard. Figure out how many mL (round to whole numbers) equal the fluid ounces listed and then write them in the correct box below. Read the clues to find out which item each child put away and how many fluid ounces and milliliters of liquid it contained.

Clues

1. Rawlins put away neither the shampoo nor a product containing 739 mL.
2. LeeAnn put away neither the product containing 25 fl. oz. nor the glass cleaner.
3. Four different products were the one containing 399 mL, the one Cassie put away, the one containing 739 mL, and the glass cleaner.
4. The shampoo contained fewer mL than the glass cleaner, but more mL than the Jet Dry®.

	dish soap	glass cleaner	Jet Dry®	shampoo	8.45 fl. oz. mL	13.5 fl. oz. mL	25 fl. oz. mL	32 fl. oz. mL
Cassie								
LeeAnn								
Rawlins								
Wayland								
8.45 fl. oz. mL								
13.5 fl. oz. mL								
25 fl. oz. mL								
32 fl. oz. mL								

Math Logic Mysteries © Taylor & Francis Group DOI: 10.4324/9781003236498-20

That's Not My Area

Students in Mrs. Bronson's math class were asked to find the area of different rectangles. The five students who finished their assignment first could omit half of their homework, but only if they had the correct answers. Not everyone accurately multiplied length times width to find the rectangles' areas. Calculate the areas to discover who made the error and try to identify the mistake he or she made in calculating. Read the clues to each student's problem and the area he or she figured.

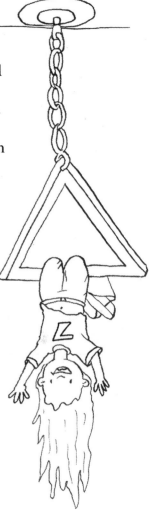

Clues

1. The one who figured the area for the 8.5 in. × 19.3 in. rectangle was neither Lily nor the student who calculated 95.16 sq. in. as the area of his or her rectangle.
2. Students who had 11.6 in. × 5.8 in. and 14.7 in. × 9.2 in. rectangles as problems did not determine 95.16 sq. in. or 164.05 sq. in. as their areas.
3. Neither Camille nor Kevan had 8.5 in. × 19.3 in., and Kevan did not have 6.1 in. × 15.6 in.
4. The student who had 7.3 in. × 12.4 in. calculated an area of 91.25 sq. in., but it wasn't Lily.
5. Evaline determined that the area of her rectangle was 135.24 sq. in., but her problem was not 11.6 in. × 5.8 in.

	7.3 in. l × 12.4 in. w	6.1 in. l × 15.6 in. w	11.6 in. l × 5.8 in. w	8.5 in. l × 19.3 in. w	14.7 in. l × 9.2 in. w	135.24 sq. in.	91.25 sq. in.	95.16 sq. in.	67.28 sq. in.	164.05 sq. in.
Camille										
Evaline										
Kevan										
Lily										
Matthew										
135.24 sq. in.					
91.25 sq. in.					
95.16 sq. in.					
67.28 sq. in.					
164.05 sq. in.					

DOI: 10.4324/9781003236498-21

Farmer's Market

Five neighborhood kids went on a Saturday morning walk to the Farmer's Market, where people sell their produce and various items they have made or grown. Each child bought different items for his or her family and spent different amounts of money. No one bought exactly the same kinds of items and no one bought one or five different kinds of items. The items were carrots at 18 cents each, flowers at $3.89 per bunch, pies at $4.50 each, potatoes at 12 cents each, and zucchini at 3 for $1. They put all the items in a wagon and towed them home. Can you find the total amount each child spent?

Clues

1. Jayma bought 2 more kinds of items than Nancie.
2. Quade purchased vegetables only. He spent less than Jayma.
3. Alonzo got a pie for his father, flowers for his mother, and 1¼ dozen carrots for his rabbit.
4. Three of the kids were the one who bought three pies and three dozen potatoes, the child who bought everything except flowers, and one who got two dozen carrots, 12 zucchini, and six pies.

BONUS: Can you figure out what combinations of items Quade and Jayma each bought?

	$11.09	$14.96	$17.82	$23.00	$35.32
Alonzo					
Ellison					
Jayma					
Nancie					
Quade					

Math Logic Mysteries © Taylor & Francis Group
DOI: 10.4324/9781003236498-22

It's a Picnic

Five kids went to a sandbar on the river for a picnic. Each bought different foods on different days and spent different amounts of money. One got 5 packages of cookies at $.76 each and 5 yogurts at $.69 each. Another bought bologna for $3.88 and 5 buns at $.65 each. A third one got milk at $2.79 and 5 bottles of juice at $.87 each. One bought 5 oranges at $.38 each and 2 bags of pretzels at $2.57 each. One got 2 bags of candy at $1.19 each and 3 packs of string cheese at $1.61 each. Calculate the totals spent on food items and write them in the matrix. Then use the clues to discover the amount each person spent and which day he or she bought his or her groceries.

Clues
1. The one who got bologna and buns shopped on Wednesday.
2. Phil did not purchase oranges and pretzels.
3. Austin shopped on Monday, but he didn't get cookies and yogurt.
4. Missy bought the beverages. She shopped the day after Glenn.
5. Someone bought oranges and pretzels on Friday.

	$	$	$	$	$	Mon.	Tues.	Wed.	Thu.	Fri.
Austin										
Dianna										
Glenn										
Missy										
Phil										
Mon.										
Tues.										
Wed.										
Thu.										
Fri.										

DOI: 10.4324/9781003236498-23

Math Logic Mysteries © Taylor & Francis Group

I Flip for Food

The Burnsville Gymnastics Club sponsored a food drive for charity last week. Kids canvassed their neighborhoods for canned and boxed nonperishable foods. Four members, including twin brothers (Cam and Payton Hillard) and sisters (Hayden and Kim Ling) noticed that their donated items each listed different weights in ounces (oz.) and grams (g) on the labels. Hayden knew that 1 ounce equaled 28.35 grams. The four gymnasts chose one item to compare. Calculate the missing weights in grams (round to the nearest whole numbers) and write them in the grid. Then use the clues to match each gymnast with the item he or she compared and its weight.

Clues
1. Kim didn't bring soup or food that weighed 326 grams.
2. Payton did not bring food that weighed 326 grams or pasta sauce.
3. The leader thanked the boy who brought 184 grams of rice mix.
4. Cam did not bring jam or food that weighed 737 grams or 539 grams.
5. The pasta sauce weighed 737 grams.

		jam	pasta sauce	rice mix	soup	26 oz. g	19 oz. g	11.5 oz. g	6.5 oz. g
	Cam								
	Hayden								
	Kim								
	Payton								
26 oz.	g								
19 oz.	g								
11.5 oz.	g								
6.5 oz.	g								

Math Logic Mysteries © Taylor & Francis Group   DOI: 10.4324/9781003236498-24

Let the Games Begin

Five students in Mr. Shriver's math class are very competitive, so he created Game Day, where he and his students timed the five competitors playing different games. Games were played individually, except L-Game®, which was played with a volunteer opponent. Use the chart below to total the times for each row, and then write them in the grid. Read the clues to discover each student's total time for five games and which game each student liked best. Who was the speediest gamer?

Clues

1. The total time of 25 min 39 s for all five games was achieved by the one whose favorite game was Krypto®, but that wasn't Shawna.
2. Bill and Nathan didn't finish with the longest time, and Nathan did not have 25 min 45 s.
3. Neither the student who liked L-Game® or the one who liked Sudoku had a total time of 25 min 48 s or the least time.
4. The one who took the longest was neither Shawna nor the one who liked L-Game® best.
5. Francie likes 24 Game® best, but she did not take the least time to finish all five games.

24 Game®	Krypto®	L-Game®	Matrix	Sudoku	Totals
2 min 26 s	3 min 14 s	6 min 18 s	5 min 36 s	8 min 05 s	
2 min 13 s	3 min 06 s	6 min 35 s	5 min 51 s	8 min 16 s	
2 min 08 s	3 min 15 s	6 min 23 s	5 min 46 s	8 min 13 s	
2 min 21 s	3 min 02 s	6 min 19 s	5 min 32 s	8 min 23 s	
2 min 14 s	3 min 16 s	6 min 27 s	5 min 24 s	8 min 27 s	

Total Times ➤					24 Game®	Krypto®	L-Game®	Matrix	Sudoku
Bill									
Francie									
Nathan									
Shawna									
Tyler									
24 Game®									
Krypto®									
L-Game®									
Matrix									
Sudoku									

Name: Date:

Hit the Road

Five kids from Sienna tracked the miles driven for two trips their families made last summer. Complete the mileage chart. Convert fractions to decimals, and then multiply by the distance from Sienna to the city indicated. For example, ⅜ of the distance to Fowler would be .375 (⅜) × 1,782 (distance to Fowler) = 668 mi. Round to the nearest whole number. In the matrix, write the city above its correct number of miles from Sienna. Read the clues to discover which two cities each family visited. Total the mileage for each family's trips. Which family drove the farthest?

Clues

1. Of Abby and Jantzen's families, one drove to Brock and the other drove to Koty. Neither family visited Chalsy or Pattin.
2. Milea loves to visit her cousins in Fowler every summer. Milea's family didn't go to Dana, but one family visited both Dana and Chalsy.
3. Clayton's family did not go to Pattin, but the Pattin visitors also drove to Ria.
4. For one trip, Jantzen's family drove ⅞ as far as Milea's family drove on their second trip, and Abby's family drove ⅚ as far on one trip as Milea's family drove on their first trip.

Mileage Chart—Sienna to each city. (Hint: Albion is ⅞ distance to Ogden. Figure Ogden first.)

Albion	Brock	Chalsy	Dana	Fowler	Koty	Milan	Ogden	Pattin	Ria
			1,683	1,782					
⅞ of dist. to Ogden	⅚ of dist. to Fowler	11/12 of dist. to Ria			⅘ of dist. to Brock	⅔ of dist. to Pattin	⅔ of dist. to Dana	6/7 of dist. to Koty	8/9 of dist. to Albion

Math Logic Mysteries © Taylor & Francis Group
DOI: 10.4324/9781003236498-26

Hit the Road, Continued

Cities ➤			Fowler				Dana			
Miles ➤	982	800	1,782	679	1,018	1,485	1,683	1,188	1,122	873
Abby										
Clayton										
Ivy										
Jantzen										
Milea										
1,485 mi.										
1,683 mi.										
1,188 mi.										
1,122 mi.										
873 mi.										

Yearn to Learn the Pattern?

Jessa, Kyann, and Zoey are homeschooled by their father. One morning, he presented each girl with three math problems. Each was to observe the numbers, figure out the pattern and write what number would come next. Complete their chart and then transfer the numbers to the correct spaces in the Answers row of the matrix. Also, fill in the Patterns row (for example, you could write the pattern "times 6 minus 2" as "× 6 – 2"). Finally, enter missing digits in the clues. You need this information to solve the matrix. Read the completed clues and determine which three patterns each daughter finished.

Clues

1. Kyann found ___6 as an answer and solved a problem that had + 9 as part of the pattern, but she didn't solve a problem with ___0___ as the answer.

2. The problem with ___8___ was solved alongside a problem with a pattern containing a fraction, but it wasn't the problem with + 9 as part of the pattern or a problem that Zoey solved.

3. One of Jessa's answers was ___8. She didn't solve one with zero as a middle digit.

Math Logic Mysteries © Taylor & Francis Group

Yearn to Learn the Pattern?, Continued

4, 12, 24, 72, 144, 432, _____	6, 14, 7, 15, 7½, 15½ , _____	81, 64, 70, 53, 59, 42, _____
3, 18, 24, 144, 150, 900, ____	12, 21, 45, 54, 78, 87, _____	17, 9, 45, 37, 185, 177, _____
2, 7, 14, 19, 38, 43, _____	7, 21, 25, 75, 79, 237, _____	5, 15, 11, 33, 29, 87, _____

Patterns ➤ (+ 9___)   (___ − 4)

Answers ➤ ___6   7___   ___6___   ___8   __8___   __0___

Jessa

Kyann

Zoey

___8___

___0___

___ − 4

___6___

___8

+ 9___

Tri to Solve This

Mr. Pravek summoned his three sons to the garage to help him measure and cut three triangles for a woodworking project. The largest triangle had a base of 11 ¾ in. and a height of 9 ⅘ in., the middle triangle had a base of 10 ⅜ in. and a height of 8 ⁵⁄₁₆ in., and the smallest triangle had a base of 4 ⁷⁄₁₆ in. and a height of 7 ¼ in. Mr. Pravek asked each boy to guess the area of each triangle. Calculate the areas using the formula ½(b × h). Change fractions to decimals (divide the numerator by the denominator) before multiplying. Round to the nearest hundredth. Write the square inches in the Areas row. Use the clues to find which boy guessed which area for each triangle. Who guessed closest to correct?

Clues

1. The boy who guessed 55.75 sq. in. also guessed 16.75 sq. in., but not 41.5 sq. in.
2. The son who estimated 52.4 sq. in. also guessed 44.4 sq. in, but not 15.9 sq. in.
3. Ivan took a wild guess at 41.5 sq. in., but he didn't think of 55.75 sq. in.
4. Tevye was not the boy who guessed 55.75 sq. in. and 40.85 sq. in.

Areas ➤	Largest: _____ sq. in.			Middle: _____ sq. in.			Smallest: _____ sq. in.		
Sq. In. ➤	60.8	55.75	52.4	44.4	41.5	40.85	18.1	16.75	15.9
Boris									
Ivan									
Tevye									
18.1									
16.75									
15.9									
44.4									
41.5									
40.85									

 Math Logic Mysteries © Taylor & Francis Group   DOI: 10.4324/9781003236498-28

Common Cents Shopping

Three girls (Audrey, Felicity, and Tiffany) and two boys (Darion and Jake) emptied their piggy banks, stuffed the coins and bills into their pockets, and headed to the mall to make special purchases for a friend's birthday. Each child spent the least amount of units possible. For example, $1.62 is 5 units: one $1 bill, one 50-cent piece, one dime, and two pennies. Write how many units each purchase required, and then read the clues to discover how much money each child spent on which item. Note: None of the children used $2 bills, but they did use 50-cent pieces.

Clues

1. Felicity used 11 units to buy either a new ball or DVD.
2. The boys used 9 units at the check-out register, and Darion bought either the new game or a T-shirt.
3. Audrey spent $1.55 more on a new DVD or earrings than the one who purchased the new ball.
4. Jake spent $1.55 more for a game or DVD than Audrey spent.
5. Tiffany spent $1.55 more for earrings than the one who bought a T-shirt.

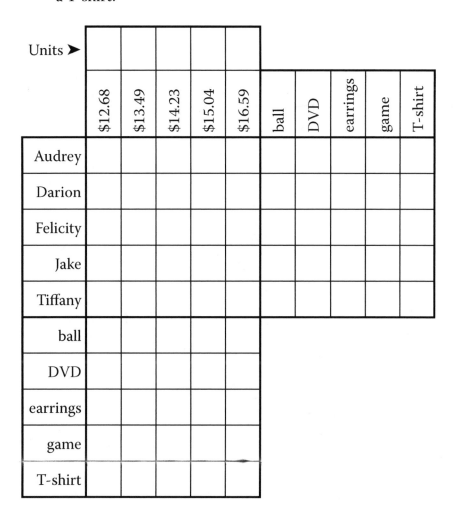

Units ▶	$12.68	$13.49	$14.23	$15.04	$16.59	ball	DVD	earrings	game	T-shirt
Audrey										
Darion										
Felicity										
Jake										
Tiffany										
ball										
DVD										
earrings										
game										
T-shirt										

That's Not Probable

Four friends were at James' house one day when Theo flipped a penny that was in his pocket. Shawn said, "I bet you can't get three heads flipping three different pennies." That was challenge enough for Theo, so he tried it. He didn't get three heads. The boys started talking about odds and decided to experiment with probability. For example, the probability (P) of getting one head with one penny is 1 of 2 (½, .5, or a ratio of 1:2) because one out of two possible outcomes is heads (H) and the other is tails (T). The P of 1H with two pennies is 2 of 4 (¾, .5, or a ratio of 2:4) because two of four possible outcomes have one head: HT and TH. Each boy flipped pennies and tried for different outcomes. Write all possible outcomes in the chart on p. 39 and calculate decimals for the ratios on the matrix. Use the information from the chart and read the clues to find which boy had which odds.

Clues

1. Theo tried to get two heads on three pennies. His odds were better than Shawn's.
2. James' odds were worse than Haru's, and Theo's were better than Adam's.
3. Adam hoped for four heads on five pennies. His odds were half as good as Shawn's.

Math Logic Mysteries © Taylor & Francis Group
DOI: 10.4324/9781003236498-30

That's Not Probable, Continued

One penny	Two pennies	Three pennies	Four pennies	Five pennies
H	HH			
	HT			
	TH			
T	TT			

Decimals ➤					
Ratios ➤	3:8	4:16	6:16	5:32	10:32
Adam					
James					
Haru					
Shawn					
Theo					

As American as Apple Pie

Mrs. Emerson needed to make four apple pies for a bake sale. She needed flour, shortening, salt, and water for the crust and butter, flour, brown sugar, cinnamon, white sugar, apples, and egg whites for the pie filling. Her recipe was for one pie. She asked her three children to calculate how much of each ingredient would be required for four pies. All four peeled and sliced four apples and each cracked and separated one egg. Each child calculated and measured three of the remaining ingredients. Use the equivalents listed in Clue 1 to help you complete the Volume × 4 row for four pies before you try to solve the matrix. Which three ingredients did each child measure?

Clues

1. 3 t. or tsp. = 1 T. or Tbsp.; 6 T. = ⅜ cup; 16 T. = 1 cup; 1 c. = 8 oz.; 4 c. = 1 quart
2. The one who calculated the measurement for white sugar was neither Hank nor the child who measured out ½ cup of a filling ingredient.
3. One child figured out he or she would need 1½ cups of one ingredient and 9 cups of another ingredient. A different child realized he or she would need 3 cups of one ingredient and 1 T. of another ingredient.
4. Marvin discovered he would need 1 T. of one ingredient for the crust, but he was not the one who calculated how much butter would be needed for four pies.

	2¼ c.	6 oz.	¾ tsp.	6 T.	8 T.	2 T.	⅝ c.	¾ tsp.	⅛ qt.
Recipe Volume ➤									
Volume × 4 ➤	c.	c.	T.	c.	c.	c.	c.	T.	c.
	flour (crust)	short-ening	salt	water	butter	flour (pie)	brown sugar	cinna-mon	white sugar
Emily									
Hank									
Marvin									
brown sugar									
cinnamon									
white sugar									
water									
butter									
flour (pie)									

People Think I'm Square

Six mathematically astute students were asked to teach their peers about square roots and square numbers. They said, "Square roots are factors that are multiplied by themselves to yield a number. For example, 3 is the square root of 9, or 3 × 3 is 9, so 9 is the square number." They practiced with 5 as the square root of 25 and 7 as the square root of 49. To find square roots, they entered a number on a calculator, and then hit the square root key (√). The peer teachers each chose a secret square number. With some helpful clues, classmates had to deduce what numbers the peer teachers had chosen. Calculate the square roots of the numbers below and write them in the boxes on the grid, and then read the clues to discover which peer teacher chose which square number.

Clues

1. Lavani said her square number was not the smallest or largest.
2. Pete said, "My square number is ¼ of Shelley's square number."
3. Garth hinted, "My square root is ½ of Alan's."
4. Lavani's square root and square number are both multiples of 9.
5. Mardell said, "My square number is a multiple of 3." Hint: Add the digits. If the sum is evenly divisible by 3, then the number is a multiple of 3 (using 162 as an example: 1 + 6 + 2 = 9).
6. Shelley said, "My square root is larger than Lavani's but smaller than Mardell's."

Square Root ➤						
Square Number ➤	256	441	729	1,024	1,296	1,764
Alan						
Garth						
Lavani						
Mardell						
Pete						
Shelley						

DOI: 10.4324/9781003236498-32   *Math Logic Mysteries* © Taylor & Francis Group   41

I'm Sittin' Good, Baby!

Three sisters love to babysit. Each girl secured three sitting assignments last Friday, Saturday, and Sunday. Each job was for a different length of time and for nine different families. Use the times on the chart to calculate how many hours and minutes each girl babysat each day. Write the lengths in the Sit Time row and beneath the names. Read the clues, mark the jobs for each girl each day, and then add the durations for each girl's jobs to discover who babysat the longest.

Clues

1. Brooke sat almost 7 hours one evening, but never started sitting at 5:25 p.m.
2. One sat from 11:46 a.m. to 3:10 p.m. on Sunday and for 5 hours and 47 minutes another day, but she didn't sit for nearly 6 hours Saturday night.
3. Brandie wasn't the one who sat from 6:56 p.m. to 12:27 a.m. on Friday and 5 hours and 56 minutes another day.
4. Brianne wasn't the sister who sat about 4 ½ hours one day and nearly 3 hours another day.

		Friday			Saturday			Sunday		
Start Time ➤		5:25 p.m.	6:18 p.m.	6:56 p.m.	9:23 a.m.	1:39 p.m.	5:20 p.m.	11:46 a.m.	2:15 p.m.	4:26 p.m.
End Time ➤		11:12 p.m.	10:47 p.m.	12:27 a.m.	4:18 p.m.	7:55 p.m.	11:16 p.m.	3:10 p.m.	5:43 p.m.	7:18 p.m.
Sit Time ➤		hr min	hr min	hr min	hr min	hr min	hr min	hr min	hr min	hr min
	Brandie									
	Brianne									
	Brooke									
Sunday										
Sunday										
Sunday										
Saturday										
Saturday										
Saturday										

 Math Logic Mysteries © Taylor & Francis Group   DOI: 10.4324/9781003236498-33

Check, Please!

On Wednesday afternoon five kids were sent to the supermarket by their parents to pick up a few necessary items. The items were pizza at $5.99, milk at $2.58 per gallon, bread at $2.04 per loaf, laundry soap at $6.23, and chips at $2.99. After finding the items, each child headed to the checkout. There was only one lane open, so everyone had to wait in the same line. Fortunately, each child only had a few items, so checking proceeded quickly. Can you determine how much each child spent and the place he or she had in line?

Clues

1. Jermain was first in line. The one who purchased two pizzas, two gallons of milk, and chips was not third.
2. Roger was second in line, but he didn't pick up a pizza, a gallon of milk, two loaves of bread, and chips.
3. The fourth person in line was not sent for three pizzas. Autumn was not third.
4. Monique got chips, two pizzas, and two gallons of milk. Jermain got only milk and soap.
5. The fifth one in line spent $20.13. Neither Autumn nor Franklin bought two loaves of bread, a pizza, a gallon of milk, laundry soap, and a bag of chips.

	1st	2nd	3rd	4th	5th	$8.81	$15.64	$17.97	$20.13	$21.87
Autumn										
Franklin										
Jermain										
Monique										
Roger										
$8.81					
$15.64					
$17.97					
$20.13					
$21.87					

DOI: 10.4324/9781003236498-34

Amassing My Fortune

Five friends collected birthday money, money from jobs, and coins found around the house that their parents said they could have. They wanted to walk to the bank and deposit their fortunes, but each child was busy with activities, so nobody could go at the same time. Total the amounts for each row of the chart. Write the totals in the matrix. Read the clues to discover how much money each child deposited and what time he or she was at the bank.

Clues

1. Someone deposited $39.96 three hours before Marlowe deposited hers.
2. Sean deposited money one hour before one of the two girls deposited $48.32.
3. Kasey deposited her money one hour after the boy who took $45.87 to the bank.
4. Someone deposited $53.65 an hour before Justin. A boy was the last to make a deposit.

Math Logic Mysteries © Taylor & Francis Group   DOI: 10.4324/9781003236498-36

Amassing My Fortune, Continued

babysitting	birthday	odd change	paper route	shovel snow	totals
$7.00	—	$1.38	$31.58	—	$
—	$19.50	$2.88	$19.49	$4.00	$
$7.50	—	$2.64	$34.93	$3.25	$
$11.50	$35.00	$1.65	—	$5.50	$
—	$17.75	$1.81	$28.35	—	$

	$	$	$	$	$	10 a.m.	11 a.m.	12 p.m.	1 p.m.	2 p.m.
Bart										
Justin										
Kasey										
Marlowe										
Sean										
10 a.m.										
11 a.m.										
12 p.m.										
1 p.m.										
2 p.m.										

It's Not a Rectangle Number

Math teacher, Ms. Whittley, explained that to square a number, you must multiply it by itself (for example, 5×5 or $5^2 = 25$). A square root is the number that was multiplied (for example, square root of 81 or $\sqrt{81} = 9$). Students squared fractions (for example, $\frac{2}{3}^2$ or $\frac{2}{3} \times \frac{2}{3} = \frac{4}{9}$) and decimal equivalents (for example, $\frac{2}{3} = .666$, so $.666 \times .666 = .444$ or $\frac{4}{9}$). Ms. Whittley assigned each student a different fraction. Each student calculated the decimal equivalent, and then multiplied the number by itself to find its square. To find decimal square roots, they entered the decimal on a calculator, and then hit the square root key. To solve this matrix, find the missing squares and square roots. Fill them in. Read the clues to determine which fraction (and its decimal equivalent) was assigned to each student. Note: You may have to convert some of the fractions to decimal equivalents to solve the problem.

Clues

1. Brittin was not the one who calculated that the decimal equivalent square of $\frac{3}{11}$ was .074.
2. Three cousins in the class are the one who was assigned $\frac{5}{8}$, the one who determined that .213 was a square, and Gloria.
3. Leiko and the one who was assigned $\frac{7}{12}$ (who isn't Gloria) are neighbors of the student whose fraction has a decimal equivalent of .074 (who also isn't Gloria).
4. Four students are the one who found .213 as a square, Brittin, the one who was assigned $\frac{6}{7}$, and Phillip.
5. Fred was not assigned $\frac{5}{8}$, but he calculated .340 as a square.

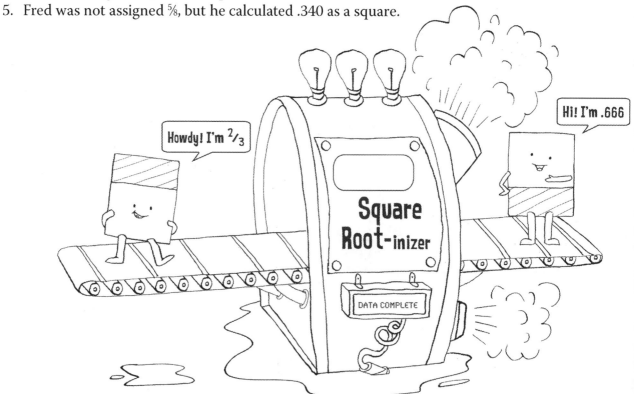

Math Logic Mysteries © Taylor & Francis Group   DOI: 10.4324/9781003236498-37

It's Not a Rectangle Number, Continued

		Fractions					Decimals				
		$\frac{5}{8}$	$\frac{6}{13}$		$\frac{7}{12}$		.857		.625		.462
sq. root ►		$\frac{25}{64}$		$\frac{36}{49}$		$\frac{9}{121}$	.734	.074		.340	
square ►											
Brittin											
Fred											
Gloria											
Leiko											
Phillip											

.857	.734					
	.074					
.625						
	.340					
.462						

The Brainy Bunch

Together five friends (three girls named Anesha, Ella, and Isanti, and two boys named David and Gregory) earned a total of 30 A's on their school report cards. Their last names are Bremer, Fay, Hardin, Polk, and Story. The percentages of A's are 13%, 17%, 20%, 23%, and 27%. Calculate to find the number of A's that equal each percentage. Round each to the nearest whole number. For example, 6% of 30 A's would be .06 × 30 = 1.8 or 2 A's. Write the number of A's in the empty spaces on the grid. Write them in the same order left to right on top, and going down beneath the names. Determine each student's first and last name and how many A's he or she earned.

Clues
1. Gregory got one more A than David.
2. Either Gregory or Miss Story got exactly 20% of the A's.
3. Either Mr. Hardin or Isanti received 50% as many A's as Miss Polk.
4. Isanti or Ella earned about 13% of the total number of A's. One of them is Miss Polk.
5. Either David or Mr. Bremer received about 17% of the total number of A's.
6. Either Anesha or Miss Fay got about 23% of the total number of A's.

	Bremer	Fay	Hardin	Polk	Story					
Anesha										
David										
Ella										
Gregory										
Isanti										

Math Logic Mysteries © Taylor & Francis Group   DOI: 10.4324/9781003236498-38

Seven Up

Should you set out for a swim at the pool if it is 25° outside? Brrr! But, what if someone said it was 25° Celsius, not 25° Fahrenheit? Those are two different temperature scales. Seven Smith siblings (six teenagers and a 12 year old) love to swim during the summer. Some swim when it's sizzling, some select simmering, and some say the soothing 70s is supreme. To solve this situation, convert Celsius temperatures to Fahrenheit and vice versa. Round your decimal answers to the tenths place. Then study the statements and specify which sibling is suited to which degree of sunshine. Use these formulas:

When you know Fahrenheit temperature: C = ⅝ × (F° − 32).
For example, 100° F is ⅝ × (100 − 32) or ⅝ × 68 which equals 38°C.
When you know Celsius temperature: F = (⅞ × C°) + 32.
For example, 100°C is (⅞ × 100) + 32 or 180 + 32 which equals 212°F.

BONUS: Can you determine which sibling is the youngest (12 years old)?

Clues

1. Sally likes warmer temperatures than Skeeter, but cooler temperatures than Summer.
2. Sawyer prefers temperatures below 90° F. Sheldon prefers temperatures above 90° F.
3. The difference between Sawyer's Celsius temperature and Skeeter's Fahrenheit temperature is exactly 48.
4. The Celsius temperature Summer loves is half of the Fahrenheit temperature Sandy likes.
5. Seaton loves a day that is exactly the same as his body temperature.
6. The Celsius temperature Skeeter prefers is double his age.

		24°		31°		35°	
Fahrenheit ➤	70°		81°		92°		98.6°
Sally							
Sandy							
Sawyer							
Seaton							
Sheldon							
Skeeter							
Summer							

Celsius ➤

Algebar's Algebra

Miss Algebar teaches math challenge group. The boys in the group (Bancroft, Troy, Brad, and Heath) are good friends. One day, Miss A taught algebra. She explained that *n* is the unknown number. Look at this problem:

$2n + 5 = 13$

If n = 4, then

$(2 \times 4) + 5 = 13$

The value of n varies for each problem. Sometimes n is on both sides of an equation. Here's another example:

$3n + 2 = 7n - 10$

If n = 3, then

$(3 \times 3) + 2 = (7 \times 3) - 10$ or

$9 + 2 = 21 - 10$

Both sides equal 11, so n = 3 is correct. Pairs of students were assigned a problem to solve together. Can you discover which students worked together and the answer they got? Solve for n in the algebra problems as you find them in the clues.

Clues

1. Five students who did not work together are Samantha, Bancroft (who did not get 5 as an answer with his partner), the one who did $2n + 3 = 4n - 1$, the girl who was paired with Dixie, and the one who solved $3n + 4 = 8n - 1$ (who wasn't Thea).
2. Neither Bancroft nor Heath did $n + 6 = 3n$, and Samantha did not solve $3n - 6 = n + 4$.
3. Blythe and Heath worked together, but did not do this problem: $3n - 6 = n + 4$.
4. The boy who worked with Misty thought $4n - 8 = 2n$ was easy to solve for n.
5. The girl who got the answer for $n + 6 = 3n$ did not work with Thea.

That's where "N" lives. Nobody's seen him.

Algebar's Algebra, Continued

	n = 1	n = 2	n = 3	n = 4	n = 5	Brad	Dixie	Heath	Misty	Thea
Ainsley										
Bancroft										
Blythe										
Samantha										
Troy										
Brad										
Dixie										
Heath										
Misty										
Thea										

Coin Club

Three boys (Drew, Ned, and Quinton) and two girls (Polly and Fedara) started the Numismatist Club. Each member collects only one denomination. No one's first name, last name, or denomination starts with the same letter. The chart shows the total cents in each collection. Mark "yes" or "no" if it is possible to make the total cents with each denomination. For example, 2,365 cents ÷ 5 cents = 473 cents, and because it divides evenly, it is "yes." The dimes row has been marked for you. Figure out which total cents goes with each coin denomination, and then write the total cents in the empty spaces on the matrix by its correct denomination. Read the clues to determine each collector's first and last name and which coin denomination he or she collects.

Clues

1. Neither Quinton nor Mr. Penne has 2,600 cents or 2,498 cents.
2. Polly has either 2,590 cents or 2,875 cents. Polly is not Miss Nichols, and Ned is not Mr. Quartez.
3. Mr. Dimus has either 2,365 cents or 2,875 cents, and Miss Feeftee has either 2,365 cents or 2,590 cents.

Math Logic Mysteries © Taylor & Francis Group   DOI: 10.4324/9781003236498-41

Coin Club, Continued

Total cents ➤	2,365 cents	2,498 cents	2,590 cents	2,600 cents	2,875 cents
pennies					
nickels					
dimes	no	no	yes	yes	no
quarters					
fifty-cent pieces					

		Total cents ➤							
Last names ➤	Penne	Nichols	Dimus	Quartez	Feeftee	pennies	nickels	dimes	quarters	fifty-cent pieces
Polly									
Ned									
Drew									
Quinton									
Fedara									
pennies									
nickels									
dimes									
quarters									
fifty-cent pieces									

The Calendar Kids

Ronald McDonald Houses work with recycling centers to get money for tabs from aluminum cans. Students saved tabs and brought them the last week of school. Six students collected tabs for years and turned in a remarkable number of them. The boys (August and March) also recycle cans. Match each student with his or her last name and the number of tabs collected. The clues require some calculations to solve. For example, to calculate 7% more than 108,000, multiply 107% or 1.07 × 108,000 = 115,560. To calculate 7% fewer than 108,000, multiply 93% (7% less than 100%) or .93 × 108,000 = 100,440.

Clues

1. June had 4% fewer tabs than Miss Weekes, who turned in 112,500 tabs.
2. Mr. Dayton had collected 2% more tabs than January.
3. Miss Yearling amassed 3% fewer tabs than January, but more than Miss Dailey.
4. August brought 3% more tabs than June.
5. Mr. Dayviss had more tabs than May, but fewer tabs than March.

	Dailey	Dayviss	Dayton	Munthley	Weekes	Yearling	108,000	109,125	111,240	112,500	113,490	114,750
April												
August												
January												
June												
March												
May												
108,000						
109,125						
111,240						
112,500						
113,490						
114,750						

Math Logic Mysteries © Taylor & Francis Group

DOI: 10.4324/9781003236498-42

Fill It Up!

Seven families stopped at gas stations to fill their cars' tanks before leaving on trips. Each driver asked his or her children to keep track of the mileage. Each car was driven a different distance, used a different amount of gas, and got different miles per gallon (mpg). After returning home, the tanks were filled again. To calculate the miles per gallon for their trips, the children divided the number of miles driven by the number of gallons of gas used. As you read the clues, jot notes in the margins, fill in the miles and gallons, do calculations, and determine each car's mpg.

Clues

1. The Riley family used 15 gallons of gas in their red Gadillac, but did not get 27 mpg.
2. Neither the Doyota nor the blue Folkswagen got 22 mpg or drove 351 miles.
3. The Marston family was very pleased to get 31 mpg on their 434-mile trip, but they did not drive the Shevvy Shaker or Todge Traveler. The Todge was driven 384 miles.
4. The Hercedes Hurrier was driven 180 miles and used 12 gallons of gas.
5. One family drove 468 miles and used 18 gallons of gas, one family drove 437 miles and used 23 gallons of gas, and one family drove a Shevvy. None of them drove a Bontiac.
6. The family that drove the Bontiac used 14 gallons of gas, the blue car used 23 gallons of gas, the car that got 24 mpg used 16 gallons of gas, and the red car got 22 mpg.

	mi.	mi.	mi.	mi.	mi.	mi.	mi.
	gal.	gal.	gal.	gal.	gal.	gal.	gal.
	15 mpg	19 mpg	22 mpg	24 mpg	26 mpg	27 mpg	31 mpg
Bontiac Bullet							
Doyota Dasher							
Folkswagen Flit							
Gadillac Gallop							
Hercedes Hurrier							
Shevvy Shaker							
Todge Traveler							

DOI: 10.4324/9781003236498-43   *Math Logic Mysteries* © Taylor & Francis Group

PARdon Moi

The Zeller family spent last evening at their favorite nine-hole golf course. Coincidentally, each player made par exactly three times. Each one also shot birdies (one under par), bogies (one over par), double bogies (two over par), and/or triple bogies (three over par). The scorecard shows results from some holes. Read the clues, deduce the missing numbers, enter them on the card, and add the scores on each hole to find the total scores. Use the chart to tally how many birdies and bogies each golfer made on nine holes. The tally chart can help you fill in some of the gaps on the scorecard, as well. Who won this game (lowest score)?

Clues

1. Sarah made par on even-numbered holes. Carroll and Paul made par on odd-numbered holes. Nobody made par on Holes 1 or 8, and someone's total for the game was 47.
2. Jeane got two birdies, a bogie, double bogies on Holes 5 and 8, and a triple bogie on 7.
3. Jeramie made par on consecutive holes. He shot four bogies and two double bogies.
4. Paul shot two bogies, three double bogies, and he had a birdie on hole 1.
5. Three golfers were the one who had triple bogies on holes 1, 5, and 8; the one who made birdies on the par 5 holes; and the one who got triple bogies on holes 4 and 8.

Math Logic Mysteries © Taylor & Francis Group

DOI: 10.4324/9781003236498-44

PARdon Moi, Continued

	birdies	pars	bogies	dbl. bogies	triple bogies	holes
Carroll		| | |				9
Jeane		| | |				9
Jeramie		| | |				9
Paul		| | |				9
Sarah		| | |				9

SCORE CARD

Par ➤	5	3	4	4	3	5	3	4	4	Scores
Hole ➤	1	2	3	4	5	6	7	8	9	▼
Carroll	7					6	5			
Jeane			5	4					4	
Jeramie		5		6			3			
Paul		5			5	7				
Sarah			6				5		6	

Time for Chapter 12

It's Chapter 12 in the math book; time for algebra! Mr. Choi assigns problems for five students to peer teach. The boys, Pierce and Ross, are nervous about getting up in front of the class, but Mr. Choi reassures them. The students will explain how to do problems such as $8n - 3 = 13$ in a way their peers will understand. They might say, "Do whatever you want, as long as you do it on both sides of the equation. You don't want $- 3$, so add 3 to both sides. Now, 8 times some number (n) + 0 is 16, so n equals 2, and then check your answer: $16 - 3 = 13$. Get it?" Solve the five algebra problems and write the correct answers in the grid. Find out which problem each student will peer teach and the day he or she will teach it.

Clues

1. Mady will teach the day before the student who will show how to solve $5n + 6 = 31$.
2. The final peer teacher will not be a boy. Neither boy will show how to solve $3n - 5 = 16$.
3. The student who will peer teach how to solve $6n + 3 = 27$ will teach the day before Pierce.
4. Ross will peer teach his problem three days after the girl who teaches $4n - 6 = 34$.
5. Taleen will peer teach the day after the student who will demonstrate $7n - 2 = 54$.

	n =	n =	n =	n =	n =	Mon.	Tue.	Wed.	Thu.	Fri.
Gabbi										
Mady										
Pierce										
Ross										
Taleen										
Mon.										
Tue.										
Wed.										
Thu.										
Fri.										

Math Logic Mysteries © Taylor & Francis Group   DOI: 10.4324/9781003236498-45

See You on the Winner's Stand

Students at Southdale School spent months designing and finishing items to enter in the school art contest. Amazingly, seven students (three girls named Alli, Evey, and Jess, and four boys named Chad, Kole, Mory, and Owen) each received the same place on all the items they entered in the contest. Can you discover how many items each student made and the place he or she earned on the items? *Note:* A small number denotes a high rank (first is high) and a large number denotes a low rank (seventh is low).

Clues

1. Alli placed lower than Evey and Owen, but higher than Jess and Kole.
2. One girl got third place on all eight of her items, and one girl got first place on all four of her items.
3. The number of items Mory made is three more than the number that is his place, and the number of items Kole made is one more than the number that is his place.
4. The number of items Owen made is four more than the number that shows his place, and the number of items Jess made is four less than the number that shows her place.
5. Owen ranked three places higher than Chad and made three times as many items as Chad.

	Number of Items Entered							Place Earned on All Items						
	2	3	4	5	6	8	9	1st	2nd	3rd	4th	5th	6th	7th
Alli														
Chad														
Evey														
Jess														
Kole														
Mory														
Owen														
1st							
2nd							
3rd							
4th							
5th							
6th							
7th							

Takin' My Load on the Road

Six kids' parents are truck drivers. On Take Your Child to Work Day, kids rode along as moms (Deedra and Shanna) and dads delivered their cargoes. There were two tankers (which carry liquid), two flatbed trucks, and two semis of crops. Each trucker unloaded part of the 45,000-pound cargo at one stop and the rest at a second stop. The numbers in the chart on p. 62 show weights remaining after the first stop. Calculate percents using this formula: Weight ÷ 45,000 = % remaining, and 100% − % remaining = % delivered. Determine each driver's cargo and weight after the first stop.

Clues

1. Bubba did not drive any of these trucks: ones that hauled concrete or corn, one that delivered 39% of its load, or the one that had 36% of its cargo remaining after the first stop.
2. The moms did not drive any of these trucks: crop semis, one that delivered 15% of its cargo, or one that had 27% of its load remaining after the first stop. However, one mom did drive a tanker.
3. Wayne did not drive the tankers, a truck with 78% of its cargo remaining after the first stop, or the truck that had delivered 64% of its load at the first stop.
4. Neither Howard nor Charlie drove a flatbed or the truck that had delivered 58% of its load, but one drove a truck with 36% remaining and one drove a truck with 27% remaining.
5. The six trucks are the ones driven by Deedra and Howard, one with 36% remaining, one that delivered 58% of its load, and the trucks delivering milk and steel pipes.

 Math Logic Mysteries © Taylor & Francis Group   DOI: 10.4324/9781003236498-47

Takin' My Load on the Road, Continued

	% delivered ➤						
	% remaining ➤						

	concrete	corn	gasoline	milk	soybeans	steel pipe	12,150 lbs	16,200 lbs	18,900 lbs	27,450 lbs	35,100 lbs	38,250 lbs
Bubba												
Charlie												
Deedra												
Howard												
Shanna												
Wayne												
12,150 lbs							
16,200 lbs							
18,900 lbs							
27,450 lbs							
35,100 lbs							
38,250 lbs							

A Dozen Cousins

Three Bobolink brothers each have four sons. One couple jokingly gave their oldest son a bird first name (Robin) to go with their bird last name. The second couple chose Martin, another bird name, and a tradition began. The cousins, dubbed the "Bird Boys," actually all like ornithology. They spearheaded a fundraiser for a $45,000 aviary at school. Each boy solicited donations from one of 12 areas in town. Read the clues to discover how much money each cousin gathered from his designated area. Do the necessary calculations to complete the grid. Amounts are listed from least to most, and the totals are in dollars with no cents. Did the cousins raise enough money?

Clues

1. Brant, Coot, and Jay's areas donated $3,400; $3,700; and $4,150, while Lark, Robin, and Wren amassed $3,550; $3,880; and $3,920 in their areas.
2. Teal's area contributed just 4% less than Lark's area, Finch gathered 15% less than Robin, and Martin pulled in 12% less than Jay.
3. Thrush gathered 20% more than Wren, Mallard's area contributed 8% more than Brant's, and Jaeger's sector donated 7% more than Coot's.
4. Robin's donations totaled either $4,150 or $3,880.

	$	$	$3,400	$	$3,550	$3,700	$3,880	$3,920	$	$4,150	$	$
Brant												
Coot												
Finch												
Jaeger												
Jay												
Lark												
Mallard												
Martin												
Robin												
Teal												
Thrush												
Wren												

Math Logic Mysteries © Taylor & Francis Group

DOI: 10.4324/9781003236498-48

I'm Being Paged—Part I

Ashley Morton absolutely loves reading! Recently she read a 264-page chapter book. Her friends also just finished books (each had fewer pages than Ashley's). They were eager to discuss them. The numbers of pages in their books are written as fractions of the 264-page book. Convert the fractions to decimals (numerator ÷ denominator), and then multiply by 264. For example: $^{11}/_{12}$ = .916, and .916 × 264 = 242 pages. Write the number of pages in the empty spaces on the matrix, and then read the clues to discover the main topic and number of pages for each person's book. You will need this information for "I'm Being Paged—Part II."

Clues

1. Neither Lewsinda nor Janelle read books with ¾ as many pages as Ashley's.
2. The girl whose book had ⅜ fewer pages than Ashley's read a story about either the Big Top coming to town or a nature series about an endangered deer species.
3. The book about a thrilling soccer tournament did not have ⅔ as many pages as Ashley's.
4. Brennan's book about a rare, albino wallaby had either ⅓ or ⅙ fewer pages than Ashley's.
5. Lewsinda did not read about deer, but Janelle learned about dribbling and kicking techniques while reading her book.

	circus	deer	soccer	wallaby	pages ➤ ⅚ of 264	¾ of 264	⅔ of 264	⅝ of 264
Brennan								
Janelle								
Lewsinda								
Stan								
⅚								
¾								
⅔								
⅝								

Math Logic Mysteries © Taylor & Francis Group

I'm Being Paged—Part II

Ashley and her friends biked to the library to return the books. Four found signed notes from mischievous pals inside their backpacks saying, "Your book is hidden at the park." Each note revealed a starting point and walking sequence (in inches, yards, meters, and rods) to a mystery location. They biked to the park, walked the sequences, and found the books. To solve this puzzle, first convert all lengths to feet. For example: 1 rod = 5½ yards × 3 or 16 ½ feet. Total the distances, and then write them in the matrix. Read the clues to learn who hid whose book, where each search began, how many feet were walked, and where each book was found. Jot notes and use information from Part I to solve this matrix. You may also want to use the chart on p. 65 and the information from the previous puzzle to help you organize your thoughts.

Clues

1. The four kids were the one who began pacing so many rods away from the slide and eventually found the circus book; the student who read 220 pages and walked 266.4 feet; Brennan, who began walking from the swing set; and the one who found a book under the WWI Veterans' bench.

2. Bert wrote directions for the one who walked 293.6 ft. and read 176 pages. His book was not at a shelter house.

3. One person's directions read, "Begin at the fountain, walk 13 meters north, 5 rods east, 26 yards north, and then 756 inches west." Her book was at the base of Lookout Tower.

4. Fujita hid the book about the circus and wrote a walking sequence that totaled 203.2 feet.

5. Caela did not hide a book at the mini-golf course, nor plot a walking course that included 26 yards.

Math Logic Mysteries © Taylor & Francis Group   DOI: 10.4324/9781003236498-50

I'm Being Paged—Part II, Continued

	Starting Place	Distance Traveled	Hiding Place
Brennan			
Janelle			
Lewsinda			
Stan			

				inches ➤	408	756	852	576
12 in. =	1 foot			yards ➤	19	26	28	23
3 feet =	1 yard			meters ➤	19	13	12	17
1 meter =	1.1 yards			rods ➤	3	5	6	8
1 rod =	5 ½ yards							
	start at fountain	start at swing set	start at pool	start at slide	ft.	ft.	ft.	ft.
Bert								
Caela								
Fujita								
Raman								
ft.								
ft.								
ft.								
ft.								

Pop 'N Zip

One evening the Jones family was browsing through their atlas when they discovered towns in six different states that were the same names as their six sons (Craig, Dale, Floyd, Marcus, Parker, and Scott). They compared the towns' populations from 1990 and 2000 and looked up the towns' zip codes. Can you match each town with its populations and zip code?

Clues

1. One town increased its population by 21 people in 10 years, and Parker increased by 325 between 1990 and 2000, while Dale and Marcus both decreased in population between 1990 and 2000.
2. In the 2000 census, Scott had 1,153 more than triple its 1990 population, and Craig had 343 more than double its 1990 population.
3. Neither Floyd nor Scott has the largest zip code, neither Marcus nor Craig has the 32404 zip code, and Marcus' zip code is about 44.807 times larger than its 2000 population.
4. Dale's 1990 population and zip code start with the same two numbers.
5. In 1990, the town with a population of 411 then had two numbers in common with its zip code, and in 2000, the town with a population of 7,870 then had three numbers in common with its zip code.

	1990 Population						2000 Population						Zip Code					
	411	527	1,206	1,906	2,239	4,298	432	1,139	1,397	1,503	4,623	7,870	19504	24091	32404	51035	70583	99921
Craig, AK																		
Dale, PA																		
Floyd, VA																		
Marcus, IA																		
Parker, FL																		
Scott, LA																		
19504																		
24091																		
32404																		
51035																		
70583																		
99921																		
432																		
1,139																		
1,397																		
1,503																		
4,623																		
7,870																		

Math Logic Mysteries © Taylor & Francis Group — DOI: 10.4324/9781003236498-51

Solutions

The introduction, charts, and clues contain enough information to solve each puzzle. However, if you get stuck, use the descriptions in this section to figure something out.

The descriptions below reflect the author's reasoning. You might use different thinking and still get correct solutions. The important thing is that you are using good logic and reasoning.

Teachers and parents may use the solutions to check student accuracy, or students may self-check their answers. Solutions are described in order of clues and display step-by-step reasoning. Correct missing information for charts and other fill-in boxes is found at the beginning of the description. A summary of correct answers is at the end of the description.

Brackets such as [2] refer to something learned in Clue 2 and the denotation (only one) means there is only one empty box horizontally or vertically. Mark the empty box with O.

You're "Bus" ted, p. 9

Clue 1: Shaman rides 4 or 5; Ryeisha rides 8 or 10.

Clue 2: Winston rides 8 or 10; Ellsworth rides 4 or 5.

Clue 3: Gina rides 12 or 15; Ellsworth rides 4 or 5.

Clue 4: Ami rides 12 or 15; Shaman rides 4 or 5.

Clue 5: The only choices left for Ryeisha and Winston are 8 and 10, but the clue says Ryeisha is lower, so she rides Bus 8 and Winston rides Bus 10.

Further Reasoning: Ryeisha rides 8, so Shaman rides 4 [1] and Ami rides 12 [4]. Winston rides 10, so Ellsworth rides 5 [2] and Gina rides 15 [3].

Answers: Ami, Bus 12; Ellsworth, Bus 5; Gina, Bus 15; Ryeisha, Bus 8; Shaman, Bus 4; Winston, Bus 10.

Card Sharks, p. 10

Clue 1: One girl had 54, 63, or 81 points (refers to "her" opponent).

Clue 2: Lukas made 81 points ($.9 \times 90$, only one that works), so Elizabeth made 90 points.

Clue 3: Walker made 63 ($.7 \times 90$).

Clue 4: Hannah had 54 ($.5 \times 108$) and Michelle had 108.

Answers: Elizabeth, 90; Hannah, 54; Lukas, 81; Michelle, 108; Walker, 63.

Frac Attack, p. 11

Decimal equivalents (L to R): .6, .607, .609, .615, .619, .625, .636.

Clue 1: Anya had the card with $^{14}/_{23}$, $^{8}/_{13}$, or $^{13}/_{21}$.

Clue 2: Titan did not have $^{17}/_{28}$, Danette did not have $^{13}/_{21}$, and neither student had $^{8}/_{13}$.

Clue 3: Guy didn't have $^{7}/_{11}$ (one larger), $^{3}/_{5}$, or $^{17}/_{28}$ (two smaller). Danette didn't have $^{3}/_{5}$, $^{17}/_{28}$, or $^{14}/_{23}$ (at least three smaller). Chachi and Titan didn't have $^{5}/_{8}$ or $^{7}/_{11}$ (two larger).

Clue 4: Anya didn't have $^{14}/_{23}$ (.609) or .619 ($^{13}/_{21}$), so she had $^{8}/_{13}$ (only one). Guy had $^{13}/_{21}$ (.619, only one).

Clue 5: Titan didn't have $^{3}/_{5}$, he had $^{14}/_{23}$ (only one). Jaquirius had $^{3}/_{5}$ or .6 (60%), so Chachi had $^{17}/_{28}$ (only one).

Clue 6: Danette had $^{5}/_{8}$; Evonne had $^{7}/_{11}$.

Answers: Anya, $^{8}/_{13}$; Chachi, $^{17}/_{28}$; Danette, $^{5}/_{8}$; Evonne, $^{7}/_{11}$; Guy, $^{13}/_{21}$; Jaquirius, $^{3}/_{5}$; Titan, $^{14}/_{23}$; Danette's and Titan's assertions were incorrect.

I Am Just a Rec, p. 12

Clue 1: Hoshi and Rhett did not answer 24.65, 30.33, 31.5, or 32.

Clue 2: Kyla's answer was not 24.5, 24.65, 29.85, 30.33, or 31.5. Rhett's answer was not 24.5 or 29.85.

Clue 3: Carlton, Fay, and Jill did not answer 24.5, 28, 30.33, or 32. Rhett did not answer 28.

Clue 4: Fay did not answer 25.75 or 31.5. Mona did not answer 24.65, 25.75, 26.4, 29.85, 31.5, or 32.

Clue 5: Carlton, Dee, Mona, and Rhett answered 24.5, 26.4, 29.85, and 31.5 sq. ft. No other students could have those answers.

Clue 6: Carlton did not answer 24.65 or 25.75. Dee did not answer 24.65, 25.75, 28, 30.33, or 32.

Further Reasoning: Mona did not answer 28 or 30.33, she answered 24.5 (only one). Rhett did not answer 24.5 [Mona] or 25.75, he answered 26.4 (only one). Then, Nash answered 30.33, Kyla answered 32, Hoshi answered 28, Jill answered 25.75, and Fay answered 24.65 (only ones). Dee did not answer 26.4 [Rhett], she answered 31.5. Carlton did not answer 26.4 [Rhett], he answered 29.85.

Answers: Carlton, 29.85; Dee, 31.5; Fay, 24.65; Hoshi, 28; Jill, 25.75; Kyla, 32; Mona, 24.5; Nash, 30.33; Rhett, 26.4; The area of the window is 31.625 square feet, so Dee was closest.

This Arm Has Charm, p. 13

Clue 1: Hallie's throw was 80 ($.5 \times 160$) or 65 ($.5 \times 130$) feet. Therefore, Chaisa's throw was 160 or 130 feet.

Clue 2: Denzel threw 130 or 160 feet. Therefore, Kirah threw 65 or 80 feet (100% farther means twice as far).

Clue 3: 75% of 160 ($.75 \times 160$) = 120, 75% of 130 = 97.5 (not a choice), 75% of 120 = 90, 75% of 90 = 67.5 (not a choice), and 75% of 80 = 60 (not a choice). Chaisa and Denzel are 160 and 130 [1, 2], so Norman's throw was not 160 feet and Yuri's throw was not 120, so the only one that works out is Norman throwing 120 feet and Yuri throwing 90 feet.

Clue 4: If Hallie threw 65 feet, then 1.5 (50% farther) × 65 = 97.5 (not a choice). If Hallie threw 80, then $1.5 \times 80 = 120$, and that is Norman's distance, so Hallie threw 80 ft.

Further Reasoning: Kirah threw 65 feet (only one). Hallie threw 80 feet, so Chaisa threw 160 feet [1]. Kirah threw 65 feet, so Denzel threw 130 feet [2].

Answers: Chaisa, 160 feet; Denzel, 130 feet; Hallie, 80 feet; Kirah, 65 feet; Norman, 120 feet; Yuri, 90 feet.

Need for Speed, p. 14

Clue 1: Ryan's speed is 8, 10, 12, or 14; Daniel's speed is 6, 8, 10, or 12; and Angela's speed is 4, 6, 8, or 10.

Clue 2: Nina's speed is 8, 10, 12, or 14; Allison's speed is 6, 8, 10, or 12; and Kelly's speed is 4, 6, 8, or 10.

Clue 3: Rachel's speed isn't 4 or 5 (faster than at least two others), so Megan's speed is 5 (only one), and Rachel's speed is 15 (only one).

Clue 4: Ryan's speed isn't 14 (no 7), so Daniel's speed isn't 12 [1], Angela's speed isn't 10 [1], and Nina's speed is 14 (only one).

Further Reasoning: Allison's speed is 12 [2], and Kelly's speed is 10 [2]. Ryan's speed is 8, Daniel's speed is 6, and Angela's speed is 4 (only ones).

Answers: Allison, 12 mph; Angela, 4 mph; Daniel, 6 mph; Kelly, 10 mph; Megan, 5 mph; Nina, 14 mph; Rachel, 15 mph; Ryan, 8 mph.

Let's Party!, p. 15

Clue 1: Costs: beans, $17.52; chips $10.76; paper items, $17.66; hamburger, $22.68; buns and condiments, $14.25; and sodas, $15.84.

Clue 2: Mareesa didn't spend $22.68 or $10.76, Victor didn't spend $10.76 or $14.25, and Jordon didn't spend $22.68 or $17.66. Cassidy didn't spend $22.68 or $10.76, Bekkah didn't spend $10.76 or $14.25, and Leonard didn't spend $22.68 or $17.66.

Clue 3: Bekkah and Leonard didn't spend $15.84 on sodas. Jordon and Victor didn't spend $17.52 on beans.

Clue 4: Victor bought the hamburger meat (only boy left). Cassidy didn't spend $17.66.

Clue 5: Leonard spent less than $15.84 (sodas) and more than $10.76 (chips), so he must have spent $14.25. Jordon bought chips for $10.76 (only one). A girl bought soda. Mareesa bought sodas, because Jordon got chips.

Further Reasoning: Cassidy bought beans and Bekkah bought paper items (only ones).

Answers: Bekkah, paper items, $17.66; Cassidy, beans, $17.52; Jordon, chips, $10.76; Leonard, buns and condiments, $14.25; Mareesa, sodas, $15.84; Victor, hamburger, $22.68; Total is $98.71.

Game Girl, p. 16

Clue 1: Anna Maria's last name isn't Drexel.

Clue 2: Macalester and Anna Maria's last names aren't Grinnell. Grinnell scored 4,500 or 3,100, Macalester scored 3,100 or 2,250, and Anna Maria scored 2,250 or 1,550.

Clue 3: Amber's last name isn't Miss Bradley. Bradley scored 1,550 or 2,250 and Amber scored 3,100 or 4,500.

Clue 4: Drexel scored 3,100 or 4,500, and Marshall scored 1,550 or 2,250.

Clue 5: Grinnell scored 4,500 or 3,100, so Macalester scored 2,250 or 1,550, but she didn't score 1,550 [2]. Macalester scored 2,250, and Grinnell scored 4,500.

Further Reasoning: Drexel scored 3,100 (only one). Macalester (2,250) can't be Drexel (3,100). Marshall scored 1,550 [4]. Bradley scored 2,250 (only one), so that's Macalester's last name (both 2,250). Then, Amber scored 4,500 [3], Anna Maria scored 1,550, and Chadron scored 3,100 (only ones). Anna Maria's last name is Marshall (1,550), Amber's last name is Grinnell (4,500), and Chadron's last name is Drexel (3,100).

Answers: Amber Grinnell, 4,500; Anna Maria Marshall, 1,550; Chadron Drexel, 3,100; Macalester Bradley, 2,250.

Model Behavior, p. 17

Clue 1: Roberto posed Tuesday, Wednesday, or Thursday, and Aleene posed Wednesday, Thursday, or Friday. The restaurant shoot occurred on Monday, Tuesday, or Wednesday. The child who posed at the restaurant is a boy, so it's not Aleene, Kristen, or Roberto (whose picture was taken the day after the restaurant shoot).

Clue 2: The zoo shoot occurred Wednesday or Thursday. The zoo shoot features a girl, so it was not Cooper, Roberto, or Sebastian. The airport shoot occurred Monday or Tuesday. Sebastian has to be Thursday or Friday, so he's not the boy at the restaurant. Cooper must be the boy at the restaurant (he's not on Thursday or Friday [1]). Aleene must have posed on Wednesday, Thursday, or Friday, so she's not the child at the airport.

Clue 3: The mall shoot was not on Monday, and the ice cream shop shoot was not on Friday. The mall shoot had to be on Friday (only one). Roberto did not pose on Friday, so he was not the child at the mall.

Clue 4: Aleene posed on Wednesday [1], because two shoots follow hers. The zoo shoot occurred on Thursday. Sebastian posed on Friday. The child at the zoo isn't Aleene, so it's Kristen [2]. Sebastian's picture was taken at the mall (both on Friday).

Further Reasoning: Aleene (Wednesday) had her picture taken at the ice cream shop and Roberto's picture was taken at the airport (only ones). Roberto posed on Tuesday (only one). The zoo shoot occurred on Thursday [2]. The restaurant shoot was on Monday [only one and 1], and Cooper posed on Monday.

Answers: Aleene, ice cream shop, Wednesday; Cooper, restaurant, Monday; Kristen, zoo, Thursday; Roberto, airport, Tuesday; Sebastian, mall, Friday.

Roundabout, p. 18

Rounding: 5,000; 6,000; 18,000; 30,000; 64,000; 74,000; 147,000; 728,000.

Clue 1: Alvin didn't have 4,559 or 5,858; Indigo didn't have 4,559 or 728,196; and Ebony didn't have 146,913 or 728,196.

Clue 2: Iva Jane didn't have one of the four smallest numbers, and Osborn didn't have one of the four largest numbers.

Clue 3: Olathe and Ebony didn't have 4-digit or 6-digit numbers, and Ewing and Uma didn't have 5-digit numbers.

Clue 4: Osborn didn't have 4,559 or 728,196 [2]; Ebony didn't have 4,559 or 5,858 [3]; and Ewing didn't have 146,913 or 728,196.

Clue 5: Alvin and Indigo have 30,499 and 63,812, so Ebony, Iva Jane, Olathe, and Osborn did not have those numbers, and Alvin and Indigo didn't have any other numbers.

Clue 6: Ewing didn't have 146,913 or 728,196 [4]. Uma didn't have 4,559 or 728,196. Iva Jane had 728,196 (only one), and Uma had 146,913 and Ewing had 4,559 (only ones).

Further Reasoning: Osborn had 5,858 (only one). Alvin had 63,812 [1], Indigo had 30,499, and Ebony had 17,681 [1]. Olathe had 74,032 (only one).

Answers: Alvin, 63,812; Ebony, 17,681; Ewing, 4,559; Indigo, 30,499; Iva Jane, 728,196; Olathe, 74,032; Osborn, 5,858; Uma, 146,913; Osborn, Alvin, Olathe, and Iva Jane rounded correctly.

Ewing rounded tens, Ebony rounded thousands and hundreds, Indigo rounded hundreds, and Uma rounded ten thousands.

20 Questions, p. 19

Clue 1: Juan did not have 10 and he must have a number 8 less than another number, so he did not have 9 (no 17), 8 (no 16), -3 (no 5), -9 (no -1), or -4 (no 4). Olivia's number is 8 more than Juan's number, so she must have 1 or 9.

Clue 2: Trent did not have a negative number or 10.

Clue 3: Effie did not have -4. She had either 1 or 8 (numbers that are cubes: $1 \times 1 \times 1 = 1$ and $2 \times 2 \times 2 = 8$).

Clue 4: Barclay did not have 1 or higher. His number is 18 less than Trent's number, so he did not have -3 (no 15), -4 (no 14), or -7 (no 11). Barclay had -9 and Trent had 9.

Clue 5: Hunan didn't have 1 or higher. His number times 3 equals 12, so his number is not -3 or -7. His number has to be -4.

Clue 6: Add 13 to -3 to equal 10, so Kelci had -3 and Merrick had 10.

Further Reasoning: Olivia had 1 (only one), so Juan had -7 [1]. Effie had 8 (only one).

Answers: Barclay, -9; Effie, 8; Hunan, -4; Juan, -7; Kelci, -3; Merrick, 10; Olivia, 1; Trent, 9.

Cash for Camp, p. 20

Clue 1: Esther and Jacque did not pay 15×2 ($30) or 30×2 ($60), or hire Jaleesa for mowing. Mowing didn't earn $30 or $60.

Clue 2: Linda did not hire Jaleesa for laundry; Linda paid 20×2 ($40) or 10×2 ($20) and laundry earned 20×2 ($40) or 10×2 ($20), so neither are $30, $50, or $60.

Clue 3: Chondra and Jacque did not pay 25×2 ($50) or 20×2 ($40). Chondra and Jacque did not hire Jaleesa for painting, and painting did not earn $50 or $40. Jacque paid $20 (only one), but did not hire Jaleesa for mowing or painting, so $20 was not paid for mowing or painting. Linda paid $40 (only one), and Esther paid $50 (only one). Esther did not hire Jaleesa for mowing, so mowing did not earn $50. Mowing earned $40 (only one). Linda paid $40, so she hired Jaleesa for mowing. Laundry earned $20 (only one) and Jacque paid $20, so she hired Jaleesa for laundry. Painting did not earn $50, so Esther (who paid $50) did not hire Jaleesa for painting. Helene hired Jaleesa for painting (only one).

Clue 4: Dusting did not earn 25×2 ($50) or 30×2 ($60), so it's $30 (only one).

Further Reasoning: Painting (Helene) earned $60 and weeding earned $50 (only ones). Esther hired Jaleesa for weeding (both $50). Chondra hired Jaleesa for dusting (only one).

Answers: Chondra, dusting, $30; Esther, weeding, $50; Helene, painting, $60; Jacque, laundry, $20; Linda, mowing, $40.

It's Off to Work We Go, p. 21

Times: 8:32 a.m.–5:17 p.m. = 8 hours, 45 minutes; 10:24 p.m.–7:43 a.m. = 9 hours, 19 minutes; 7:51 a.m.–4:18 p.m. = 8 hours, 27 minutes; 3:16 p.m.–12:59 a.m. = 9 hours, 43 minutes; 6:39 a.m.–4:11 p.m. = 9 hours, 32 minutes.

Clue 1: Devin's dad works from 7:51 a.m.–4:18 p.m., but he is not the nurse. The nurse did not work from 7:51 a.m.–4:18 p.m.

Clue 2: The gardener worked from 6:39 a.m.–4:11 p.m., so Devin's dad isn't the gardener.

Clue 3: The dentist worked from 8:32 a.m.–5:17 p.m. The dentist is not Marley or Devin's dad.

Clue 4: Jacy's dad is the janitor, so Devin's dad is the carpenter (only one). Jacy's dad works from 3:16 p.m.–12:59 a.m. (9 hours, 43 minutes is 11 minutes more than 9 hours, 32 minutes, which is how long Georgia's dad worked.) Georgia's dad worked from 6:39 a.m.–4:11 p.m.

Further Reasoning: The nurse worked from 10:24 p.m.–7:43 a.m. (only one). Marley's dad worked from 10:24 p.m.–7:43 a.m. (only one), so her dad is a nurse. Georgia's dad worked from 6:39 a.m.–4:11 p.m., so he's a gardener. Elaine's dad is a dentist (he worked from 8:32 a.m.–5:17 p.m.).

Answers: Devin, 7:51 a.m.–4:18 p.m., carpenter; Elaine, 8:32 a.m.–5:17 p.m., dentist; Georgia, 6:39 a.m.–4:11 p.m., gardener; Jacy, 3:16 p.m.–12:59 a.m., janitor; Marley, 10:24 p.m.–7:43 a.m., nurse.

The Quad Squad, p. 22

Clue 1: The arrest on Monty Road only could have occurred at 2:44 a.m., therefore Kyra made her arrest at 4:48 p.m. Kyra did not make her arrest on Monty Road.

Clue 2: The arrest on Lindner Terrace only could have occurred at 4:54 a.m., therefore Sabrina made her arrest at 4:14 p.m. Sabrina did not make her arrest on Lindner Terrace.

Clue 3: Debra made her arrest at 4:54 a.m., and Helena made her arrest at 2:44 a.m. Helena made her arrest on Monty Road and Debra made hers on Lindner Terrace (4:54 a.m.).

Clue 4: 3449 is lower than 4774, so the arrest made at 4:48 p.m. occurred on Hunter Ave. Kyra made her arrest on Hunter.

Further Reasoning: Sabrina (4:14 a.m.) made her arrest on North 24th Street (only one).

Answers: Debra, 4046 Lindner Terrace, 4:54 a.m.; Helena, 4418 Monty Road, 2:44 a.m.; Kyra, 3449 Hunter Avenue, 4:48 p.m.; Sabrina, 4774 North 24th Street, 4:14 p.m.

He's Far, Far Away, p. 23

Clue 1: The only number that divides evenly into fifths is 60, and ⅘ of 60 feet is 48 feet, so Mitchell's car traveled 60 feet and Jack's car traveled 48 feet.

Clue 2: Denton's car did not travel as far as Alabaster's car. Alabaster could be 51 feet, but ¾ of 51 feet (.75 × 51) equals 38 ¼ feet, which is not an option. Alabaster's car could be 54 feet, but ¾ of 54 feet equals 40 ½ feet, which is not an option. Alabaster's car could also be 56 feet and ¾ of 56 feet equals 42 feet. That is the only one that works out, so Denton's car traveled 42 feet and Alabaster's car traveled 56 feet.

Clue 3: Jack's car traveled 48 feet, and ⅛ of 48 feet (.125 × 48) equals 6 feet, so 48 feet plus another 6 feet equals 54 feet. Perry's car traveled 54 feet.

Clue 4: Garrett's car traveled 51 ft. (only one).

Answers: Alabaster, 56 ft.; Denton, 42 ft.; Garrett, 51 ft.; Jack, 48 ft.; Mitchell, 60 ft.; Perry, 54 ft.

The Octagon, p. 24

Clue 1: Jackson's room is across from Vince's room, Efrem's room is across from Orvil's room.

Clue 2: There is one room between Curtis and Vince and one room between Arvin and Orvil.

Clue 3: Hakeem's room is next to Vince's room, and Clint's room is next to Arvin's room.

Clue 4: Clint's room is on the south corner [Introduction says the south gets the most sun], so Arvin's room is either SW or SE [3], making Orvil's room NW, NE, SW, or SE [2] and Efrem's room SE, SW, NE, or NW [1].

Clue 5: Jackson's room is on the west corner (sun sets in the west), so Vince's room is on the east corner [1]. If Vince's room is on the east corner, then Curtis's room is N [2] and Hakeem's is NE or SE [3]. Efrem's room is is SE (sun rises in the east), so Orvil is NW [1], Arvin is SW [2], and Hakeem is NE (only one).

Answers: Arvin, SW; Curtis, N; Efrem, SE; Hakeem, NE; Jackson, W; Clint, S; Orvil, NW; Vince, E.

Math Match, p. 25

Correct Conversions: 2 ½ miles, 3 ⅛ miles, 4 ⅜ miles, 5 ⅝ miles; 8.818 pounds, 11.023 pounds, 15.432 pounds, and 19.841 pounds.

Clue 1: Pierson did not convert 7 km, 5 kg, or 7 kg, and the student who converted 7 km did not convert 4 kg.

Clue 2: Libby did not convert 5 km, 4 km, or 9 km, so she converted 7 km (only one). Akira did not convert 4 km or 5 km, so he converted 9 km. He did convert 4 kg, so you can link 9 km with 4 kg Pierson is 9 kg (only one).

Clue 3: Kesia did not convert 5 kg, so she had to have converted 7 kg (only one). Libby converted 5 kg (only one), so 7 km can be linked with 5 kg [2]. Pierson did not convert 4 km, so he had to have converted 5 km (only one). Kesia converted 4 km, and 4 km can now be linked with 7 kg (only ones).

Answers: Akira, 9 km, 4 kg (both incorrect); Kesia, 4 km (correct), 7 kg (incorrect); Libby, 7 km, 5 kg (both correct); Pierson, 5 km (incorrect), 9 kg (correct); Libby is "Math Champ" of the week.

Clean as a Whistle, p. 26

Clue 1: Rawlins did not put away shampoo or the container with 25 fl. oz., and the shampoo bottle did not contain 25 fl. oz.

Clue 2: LeeAnn did not put away the container with 25 fl. oz. or the glass cleaner, and the glass cleaner bottle did not contain 25 fl. oz.

Clue 3: Cassie did not put away the bottle containing 399 mL (or 13.5 fl. oz.) or the bottle containing 739 mL (or 25 fl. oz.). Cassie did not put away the glass cleaner. The glass cleaner's bottle did not contain 13.5 fl. oz. or 25 fl. oz. Wayland put away the container with 25 fl. oz. (only one). The bottles of glass cleaner and shampoo did not contain 25 fl. oz., so Wayland did not put away glass cleaner or shampoo. Rawlins is glass cleaner (only one).

Clue 4: The Jet Dry® bottle contained 250 mL (8.45 fl. oz) or 399 mL (13.5 fl. oz), the shampoo bottle could contain 399 mL (13.5 fl. oz) or 739 mL (25 fl. oz), but Clue 1 notes that the shampoo did not contain 25 fl. oz., so it must contain 13.5 fl. oz. This means that the Jet Dry® bottle contained 8.45 fl. oz.

Further Reasoning: The glass cleaner contained 32 fl. oz. (only one). Rawlins put away the container with 32 fl. oz. (only one). The dish soap bottle contained 25 fl. oz. (only one). LeeAnn put away the container with 13.5 fl. oz. (only one), so she put away the shampoo. Cassie put away the container with 8.45 fl. oz. (only one), so she put away the Jet Dry®. Wayland put away the dish soap (only one).

Answers: Cassie, Jet Dry®, 8.45 fl. oz. (250 mL); LeeAnn, shampoo, 13.5 fl. oz. (399 mL); Rawlins, glass cleaner, 32 fl. oz. (946 mL); Wayland, dish soap, 25 fl. oz. (739 mL).

That's Not My Area, p. 27

Clue 1: Lily did not have the rectangle measuring 8.5 in. × 19.3 in. Her answer was not 95.16 sq. in. The rectangle measuring 8.5 in. × 19.3 in. was not determined to have an area of 95.16 sq. in.

Clue 2: The student with the rectangle measuring 11.6 in. × 5.8 in. did not have an answer of 95.16 sq. in. or 164.05 sq. in. The rectangle measuring 14.7 in. × 9.2 in. was not determined to have an area of 95.16 sq. in. or 164.05 sq. in.

Clue 3: Camille did not have the rectangle measuring 8.5 in. × 19.3 in. Kevan did not have the rectangles measuring 8.5 in. × 19.3 in. or 6.1 in. × 15.6 in.

Clue 4: Lily did not have the rectangle measuring 7.3 in. × 12.4 in. Her answer was not 91.25 sq. in. However, the rectangle measuring 7.3 in. × 12.4 in. was determined to have an area of 91.25 sq. in.

Clue 5: Evaline's answer was 135.24 sq. in. Evaline did not have the rectangle measuring 11.6 in. × 5.8 in., so the area of the rectangle measuring 11.6 in. × 5.8 in. was not determined to be 135.24 sq. in. The area of the rectangle measuring 11.6 in. × 5.8 in. was determined to be 67.28 sq. in. (only one).

Further Reasoning: The rectangle measuring 14.7 in. × 9.2 in. was determined to have an area of 135.24 sq. in. (only one). The rectangle measuring 8.5 in. × 19.3 in. was determined to have an area of 164.05 sq. in. (only one). The rectangle measuring 6.1 in. × 15.6 in. was determined to have an area of 95.16 sq. in. (only one). Evaline had the rectangle measuring 14.7 in. × 9.2 in. Matthew had the rectangle measuring 8.5 in. × 19.3 in. (only one), so his answer was 164.05 sq. in. Lily's answer was 67.28 sq. in. (only one), so she had the rectangle measuring 11.6 in. × 5.8 in. Kevan had the rectangle measuring 7.3 in. × 12.4 in. (only one), so his answer was 91.25 sq. in. Camille had the rectangle measuring 6.1 in. × 15.6 in. and her answer was 95.16 sq. in. (only ones).

Answers: Camille, 6.1 in. × 15.6 in., 95.16 sq. in.; Evaline, 14.7 in. × 9.2 in., 135.24 sq. in.; Kevan, 7.3 in. × 12.4 in., 91.25 sq. in.; Lily, 11.6 in. × 5.8 in., 67.28 sq. in.; Matthew, 8.5 in. × 19.3 in., 164.05 sq. in.; Kevan made the calculation error of 91.25 sq. in. It should be 90.52 sq. in. He multiplied 7.3 in. × 12.5 in. instead of 7.3 in. × 12.4 in.

Farmer's Market, p. 28

Clue 1: No one got one or five different kinds of items [Intro.], so Nancie got two kinds of items and Jayma got four kinds of items.

Clue 2: Quade got carrots, potatoes, and zucchini (three kinds, all vegetables). He didn't spend $35.32 and Jayma didn't spend $11.09.

Clue 3: Alonzo spent $4.50 for pie, $3.89 for flowers, and $2.70 for carrots or $11.09 total. Alonzo bought three different kinds of items.

Clue 4: One child spent $13.50 for pies and $4.32 for potatoes or $17.82. This child bought two different kinds of items, so he or she was not Jayma, Quade, or Alonzo. One child got four different items (this child cannot be Quade, Alonzo, or Nancie). The other child spent $4.32 for carrots, $4 for zucchini, and $27 for pies or $35.32 for three different items; this child is not Jayma. The three children here must be Ellison, Jayma, and Nancie. We know that Jayma has four different kinds of items and Nancie bought two different kinds, so Nancie must be the first child, Jayma must be the second child, and Ellison must be the third child in this clue. This means that Nancie spent $17.82 and Ellison spent $35.32

Further Reasoning: Quade spent less than Jayma [2], so he's $14.96 and Jayma is $23.

Bonus: One combination could be 15 zucchini ($5), 4 dozen potatoes ($5.76), 1½ dozen carrots ($3.24), and 2 pies ($9) for Jayma; and 5 dozen carrots ($10.80), ½ dozen zucchini ($2), and 1½ dozen potatoes ($2.16) for Quade.

Answers: Alonzo, $11.09; Ellison, $35.32; Jayma, $23.00; Nancie, $17.82; Quade, $14.96.

It's a Picnic, p. 29

Costs: Cookies and yogurt cost $7.25 ($3.80 + $3.45 = $7.25); buns and bologna cost $7.13 ($3.25 + $3.88 = $7.13); milk and juice cost $7.14 ($4.35 + $2.79 = $7.14); oranges and pretzels cost $7.04 ($1.90 + $5.14 = $7.04); and candy and cheese cost $7.21 ($2.38 + $4.83 = $7.21).

Clue 1: The child who spent $7.13 (cost of bologna and buns) shopped on Wednesday.

Clue 2: Phil did not spend $7.04 on oranges and pretzels.

Clue 3: Austin shopped on Monday, so he didn't buy bologna and buns for $7.13 [1]. Austin did not spend $7.25 on cookies and yogurt, and the child who spent $7.25 did not shop on Monday.

Clue 4: Missy spent $7.14 on milk and juice. Missy did not shop on Wednesday [1]. Missy shopped a day after Glenn, so she could not have shopped on Monday. Glenn did not shop on Friday (no day after for Missy to shop). Glenn could not have shopped on Tuesday (Missy did not shop on Wednesday) or Monday (Austin shopped on Monday). Glenn shopped on either Wednesday or Thursday, meaning Missy shopped on either Thursday or Friday, and $7.14 was spent on either Thursday or Friday.

Clue 5: The person who spent $7.04 on oranges and pretzels shopped on Friday. Phil did not buy oranges or pretzels [2], so he did not shop on Friday. Missy did not buy oranges or pretzels, so she could not have shopped on Friday. Missy shopped on Thursday (only one), meaning Glenn shopped on Wednesday [4].

Further Reasoning: Phil shopped on Tuesday, and Dianna shopped on Friday (only ones). So, Dianna spent $7.04 (both

Friday). Glenn spent $7.13 (both Wednesday). Phil spent $7.25 (only one). Austin spent $7.21.

Answers: Austin, $7.21, Monday; Dianna, $7.04, Friday; Glenn, $7.13, Wednesday; Missy, $7.14, Thursday; Phil, $7.25, Tuesday.

I Flip for Food, p. 30

Conversions: 26 oz. = 737 g; 19 oz. = 539 g; 11.5 oz. = 326 g; 6.5 oz. = 184 g.

Clue 1: Kim did not bring soup or an item weighing 326 g (11.5 oz.). The soup did not weigh 11.5 oz.

Clue 2: Payton did not bring food weighing 326 g (11.5 oz.) or pasta sauce. The pasta sauce did not weigh 11.5 oz.

Clue 3: The rice weighed 184 g (6.5 oz.). Hayden and Kim [girls, Intro.] did not bring the rice or have an item weighing 184 g. The jam weighed 11.5 oz. (only one). Kim and Payton did not bring an item weighing 11.5 oz., so they did not bring jam. Kim brought pasta sauce (only one).

Clue 4: Cam did not bring jam, so his item did not weigh 11.5 oz. Hayden brought the jam weighing 11.5 oz. (only ones). Cam also did not bring an item weighing 737 g (26 oz.) or 19 oz. He brought the rice mix weighing 6.5 oz. (184 g; only one). Payton brought the soup (only one).

Clue 5: Kim brought the pasta sauce that weighed 26 oz. The soup that Payton brought weighed 19 oz. (only one).

Answers: Cam, rice, 6.5 oz. (184 g); Hayden, jam, 11.5 oz. (326 g); Kim, sauce, 26 oz. (737 g); Payton, soup, 19 oz. (539 g).

Let the Games Begin, p. 31

Totals (top to bottom): 25 min 39 s; 26 min 01 s; 25 min 45 s; 25 min 37 s; 25 min 48 s.

Clue 1: The student whose favorite game is Krypto achieved the total time of 25 min 39 s, but it wasn't Shawna.

Clue 2: Bill and Nathan's times were not 26 min 01 s. Nathan's time wasn't 25 min 45 s.

Clue 3: The student who likes L-Game did not have a total time of 25 min 48 s or 25 min 37 s. The student who likes Sudoku did not have a total time of 25 min 48 or 25 min 37 s.

Clue 4: Shawna did not have a total time of 26 min 01 s. The student who liked L-Game did not have a total time of 26 min 01 s. Shawna's favorite game isn't L-Game. The student who liked L-Game had a total time of 25 min 45 s (only one).

Clue 5: Francie liked 24 Game best, but neither Francie nor 24 Game go with 25 min 37 s. The student who liked Matrix had a total time of 25 min 37 s (only one). Francie's total time was 25 min 48 s.

Further Reasoning: The student who liked Sudoku had a total time of 26 min 01 s (only one). Tyler had a total time of 26 min 01 s (only one), so Tyler liked Sudoku. Shawna liked Matrix (only one), so her total time was 25 min 37 s (both matrix). Then, Bill's total time was 25 min 45 s (only one), so Bill liked L-Game (both 25 min 45 s). Nathan's total time was 25 min 39 s (only one), so he liked Krypto [1].

Answers: Bill, 25 min 45 s, L-Game; Francie, 25 min 48 s, 24 Game; Nathan, 25 min 39 s, Krypto; Shawna, 25 min 37 s, Matrix; Tyler, 26 min 01 s, Sudoku.

Hit the Road, pp. 32–33

Mileages: Albion is 982 mi.; Brock is 1,485 mi.; Chalsy is 800 mi.; Koty is 1,188 mi.; Milan is 679 mi.; Ogden is 1,122 mi.; Pattin is 1,018 mi.; Ria is 873 mi.

Clue 1: Abby and Jantzen traveled 1,485 and 1,188 miles. Neither Abby nor Jantzen traveled 800 or 1,018 miles. Neither child's family traveled 1,683, 1,122, or 873 miles.

Clue 2: Milea traveled 1,782 miles. She did not travel 982; 800; 679; or 1,018 miles. Milea's family also did not travel 1,683 miles. The family who did travel 1,683 miles also traveled 800 miles on their second trip.

Clue 3: Clayton's family did not travel 1,018 miles. Ivy's family traveled 1,018 miles (only one). The family who traveled 1,018 miles also traveled 873 miles, so Ivy's family also traveled 873 miles. Clayton's family traveled 1,683 miles (only one) and 800 miles [2]. Milea's family traveled 1,122 miles (only one).

Clue 4: Milea's family traveled 1,122 miles on their second trip. Divide that by ⅞ to find that Jantzen's family traveled 982 miles on their first trip. Milea's family traveled 1,782 miles on their first trip. Divide that by ⅚ to find that Abby's family traveled 1,485 miles on one trip. Therefore, Jantzen's family traveled 1,188 miles (only one), and Abby's family traveled 679 miles (only one).

Answers: Abby, Milan (679), Brock (1, 485); Clayton, Chalsy (800), Dana (1,683); Ivy, Pattin (1,018), Ria (873); Jantzen, Albion (982), Koty (1,188); Milea, Fowler (1,782), Ogden (1,122).

Totals: Abby, 679 + 1,485 = 2,164 mi.; Clayton, 800 + 1,683 = 2,483 mi.; Ivy, 1,018 + 873 = 1,891 mi.; Jantzen, 982 + 1,188 = 2,170 mi.; Milea, 1,782 + 1,122 = 2,904 mi.; Milea's family drove the farthest.

Yearn to Learn the Pattern?, pp. 34–35

Pattern Chart (L to R), top: 864 (pattern is × 3 × 2), 7 ¾ (pattern is + 8 ÷ 2), 48 (pattern is − 17 + 6); **middle:** 906 (pattern is × 6 + 6), 111 (pattern is + 9 + 24), 885 (− 8 × 5); **bottom:** 86 (+ 5 × 2), 241 (× 3 + 4), 83 (× 3 − 4).

Matrix Blanks: Patterns (L to R): + 5 × 2; × 3 + 4; + 8 ÷ 2; × 3 × 2; − 17 + 6; + 9 + 24; − 8 × 5; × 6 + 6; × 3 − 4.

Matrix Blanks: Answers (L to R): 86; 241; 7¾; 864; 48; 111; 885; 906; 83.

Clue Blanks: 86; 906; 885; 48.

Clue 1: Kyann solved for 86. She also solved for 111 (the problem with + 9 + 24 as its pattern). She did not solve for 906. The child who answered 86 also answered 111, and but the child who answered 906 did not answer 86 and 111.

Clue 2: The problem with the answer of 885 was solved with the problem with the answer 7¾. Zoey did not solve for 885 or 7¾. Kyann did not solve for 885 or 7¾. Therefore, Jessa solved the problems with 885 and 7¾ as the answer.

Clue 3: Jessa's final problem had an answer of 48.

Further Reasoning: Zoey solved for 241 (only one) and 864 (only one). Kyann did not solve for 906, so she solved for 83 (only one), and Zoey solved for 906 (only one).

Answers: Jessa, 7¾, 48, 885; Kyann, 86, 111, 83; Zoey, 241, 864, 906.

Tri to Solve This, p. 36

Areas: Largest: 11¾ (11.75) × 9⅘ (9.8) = 115.15 ÷ 2 = 57.58 sq. in.; Medium: 10 ⅜ (10.375) × 8⁵⁄₁₆ (8.3125) = 86.24 ÷ 2 = 43.12 sq. in.; Smallest: 4⁷⁄₁₆ (4.4375) × 7 ¼ (7.25) = 32.17 ÷ 2 = 16.09 sq. in.

Clue 1: The child who guessed 55.75 also guessed 16.75. The child who guessed 41.5 did not guess 16.75 or 55.75.

Clue 2: The child who guessed 52.4 also guessed 44.4. The child who guessed 15.9 did not guess 52.4 or 44.4. Then, the child who guessed 55.75 also guessed 40.85, and the child who guessed 60.8 also guessed 41.5. The child who guessed 52.4 guessed 18.1 (only one), and the child who guessed 60.8 also guessed 15.9 (only one). The child who guessed 18.1 also guessed 44.4, the child who guessed 16.75 also guessed 40.85, and the child who guessed 15.9 also guessed 41.5.

Clue 3: Ivan guessed 41.5, so he also guessed 15.9 and 60.8.

Clue 4: Tevye did not guess 55.75, so Boris did (only one). Boris also guessed 40.85 and 16.75 (both positively linked to 55.75). Tevye guessed 52.4, 44.4, and 18.1 (only ones).

Answers: Boris, 55.75, 40.85, 16.75; Ivan, 60.8, 41.5, 15.9; Tevye, 52.4, 44.4, 18.1; Boris guessed closest on the largest triangle, Tevye was closest on the middle-sized triangle, and Ivan was closest on the smallest.

Common Cents Shopping, p. 37

Matrix Blanks: Units: $12.68 = 9 units, $13.49 = 11 units, $14.23 = 10 units, $15.04 = 6 units, $16.59 = 9 units.

Clue 1: Felicity spent $13.49 (11 units), but did not buy earrings, a game, or a T-shirt.

Clue 2: Darion and Jake (boys, Intro.) spent $12.68 and $16.59 (9 units). Audrey and Tiffany (girls, Intro.) did not spend $12.68 or $16.59. They spent $14.23 and $15.04. Darion didn't get a ball, DVD, or earrings.

Clue 3: Audrey spent $14.23, $15.04, or $16.59, but she did not spend $16.59 [2]. Then, the person who bought the ball spent $12.68 or $13.49. Audrey did not buy the ball, game, or T-shirt.

Clue 4: Jake spent $14.23, $15.04, or $16.59, but he could not have spent $14.23 or $15.04 (Audrey and Tiffany spent those amounts). Jake spent $16.59 and Audrey spent $15.04. Darion spent $12.68 (only one) and Tiffany spent $14.23 (only one).

Clue 5: Tiffany bought earrings for $14.23, so the T-shirt cost $12.68 and was bought by Darion.

Further Reasoning: Audrey bought the DVD and Jake bought the game (only ones). The ball cost $13.49 [3], which is the amount Felicity spent, so she bought the ball.

Answers: Audrey, $15.04, DVD; Darion, $12.68, T-shirt; Felicity, $13.49, ball; Jake, $16.59, game; Tiffany, $14.23, earrings.

That's Not Probable, pp. 38–39

Possible outcomes are: (three pennies) HHH, HTH, HHT, THH, TTT, THT, TTH, HTT; (four pennies) HHHH, HHTH, HHHT, HTHH, HTTT, HTHT, HTTH, HHTT, THHH, THTH, THHT, TTHH, TTTT, TTHT, TTTH, THTT; (five pennies) HHHHH, HHHTH, HHHHT, HHTHH, HHTTT, HHTHT, HHTTT, HHHTT, HHHHTT, HTHHH, HTHTH, HTHHT, HTTHH, HTTTT, HTTHT, HTTTH, HTHTT, THHHH, THHTH, THHHT, THTHH, THTTT, THTHT, THTTH,

THHTT, TTHHH, TTHTH, TTHHT, TTTHH, TTTTT, TTTHT, TTTTH, TTHTT.

Matrix Blanks: Decimals: 3:8 = .375; 4:16 = .25; 6:16 = .375; 5:32 = .16; 10:32 = .31.

Clue 1: The ratio for 2H from 3 pennies is 3:8 (.375), so Theo's odds were 3:8. Shawn's odds were worse than Theo's, so he is either 4:16, 5:32, or 10:32.

Clue 2: James' odds were not 6:16. Adam's odds were not 6:16. Haru's odds were not 5:32.

Clue 3: The ratio for 4H from 5 pennies is 5:32. Adam's odds were 5:32. Shawn's odds were 10:32 (twice as good as 5:32).

Further Reasoning: James' odds were worse than Haru's, so his odds must be 4:16, and Haru's must be 6:16.

Answers: Adam, 5:32; James 4:16; Haru, 6:16; Shawn, 10:32; Theo, 3:8.

As American as Apple Pie, p. 40

Matrix Blanks: Volume × 4 (L to R; Using Clue 1): 9 c., 3 c., 1 T., 1½ c., 2 c., ½ c., 2½ c., 1 T., 2 c.

Clue 2: Hank did not make the calculation for white sugar or for the ½ cup of flour for the pie filling. The child who calculated for ½ c. of flour for the pie filling did not also make the calculation for white sugar.

Clue 3: One child measured water and flour for the crust. One child measured shortening and cinnamon (can't be 1 T. salt, because it's in the same group as shortening).

Clue 4: Marvin calculated the 1 T. of salt for the crust. Marvin did not measure the butter, and the child who measured water did not measure salt. Therefore, Marvin measured the flour for the pie filling. The child who made the calculations for the flour for the filling did not make the calculation for the white sugar, so Marvin did not calculate for the white sugar. The child who calculated for shortening also calculated for cinnamon, so Marvin could not have made the calculation for cinnamon. Therefore, Marvin made the calculation for brown sugar.

Further Reasoning: Hank measured the cinnamon and Emily measured the white sugar (only ones). The child who measured the flour for the crust also measured the white sugar (only one). The child who measured the white sugar also measured the water. Emily measured the white sugar, so she also measured the flour for the crust and the water. Hank measured for the shortening, butter, and cinnamon (only ones).

Answers: Emily, flour (crust), water, white sugar; Hank, shortening, butter, cinnamon; Marvin, salt, flour (pie filling), brown sugar.

People Think I'm Square, p. 41

Matrix Blanks: 16, 21, 27, 32, 36, 42.
Clue 1: Lavani's number is not 256 or 1,764.
Clue 2: Pete's number is either 256 or 441. Shelley's number is either 1,024 or 1,764.
Clue 3: Garth's square root is 16 or 21. Alan's square root is 32 or 42.
Clue 4: The numbers that are multiples of 9 are 441, 279, 1,296, and 1,764. Lavani's number cannot be 1,764 [1]. However, Lavani's square root also has to be a multiple of 9, therefore, Lavani's number can only be 729 or 1,296.

Clue 5: Mardell's number is not 256 or 1,024.
Clue 6: Shelley's square root cannot be 16 or 42, so her number cannot be 256 or 1,764. Shelley's number is 1,024 [2]. Therefore, Mardell's number must be 1,296 or 1,764. If Lavani's square root is smaller than Shelley's, her square root has to be 27 and her number has to be 729. If Shelley's number is 1,024, then Pete's number must be 256 [2].

Further Reasoning: Garth's number is 441; Alan's number is 1,764; and Mardell's number is 1,296 (only ones).

Answers: Alan, 1,764; Garth, 441; Lavani, 729; Mardell, 1,296; Pete, 256; Shelley, 1,024.

I'm Sittin' Good, Baby!, p. 42

Matrix Blanks: Friday: 5 hr 47 min, 4 hr 29 min, 5 hr 31 min; **Saturday:** 6 hr 55 min, 6 hr 16 min, 5 hr 56 min; **Sunday:** 3 hr 24 min, 3 hr 28 min, 2 hr 52 min.

Clue 1: Brooke sat for 6 hr 55 min during Saturday's 9:23 a.m. to 4:18 p.m. shift. Brooke never started sitting at 5:25 p.m., so she did not sit from 5:25 p.m. to 11:12 p.m. on Friday.

Clue 2: The sister who sat from 11:46 a.m. to 3:10 p.m. on Sunday also sat from 5:25 p.m. to 11:12 p.m. on Friday. However, this sister did not sit from 5:20 p.m. to 11:16 p.m. on Saturday. Brooke did not sit from 5:25 p.m. to 11:12 p.m. on Friday, so she also did not sit from 11:46 a.m. to 3:10 p.m. on Sunday.

Clue 3: Brandie did not sit from 6:56 p.m. to 12:27 a.m. on Friday or from 5:20 p.m. to 11:16 p.m. on Saturday. Brandie sat from 1:39 p.m. to 7:55 p.m. on Saturday (only one). Brianne sat from 5:20 p.m. to 11:16 p.m. on Saturday (only one).

Clue 4: Brianne did not sit from 6:18 p.m. to 10:47 p.m. on Friday. Brooke sat during this time frame (only one). Brianne also did not sit from 4:26 p.m. to 7:16 p.m. on Sunday.

Further Reasoning: Brianne sat from 5:20 p.m. to 11:16 p.m. on Saturday. Therefore, she did not sit from 5:25 p.m. to 11:12 p.m. on Friday or from 11:46 a.m. to 3:10 p.m. on Sunday [2]. Brandie sat during these times (only one). Brianne sat from 6:56 p.m. to 12:27 a.m. on Friday and from 2:15 p.m. to 5:43 p.m. on Sunday (only one). Brooke sat from 4:26 p.m. to 7:18 p.m. on Sunday (only one).

Answers: Brandie, 5 hr 47 min (5:25 p.m. to 11:12 p.m., Friday), 6 hr 16 min (1:39 p.m. to 7:55 p.m., Saturday), 3 hr 24 min (11:46 a.m. to 3:10 p.m., Sunday); Brianne, 5 hr 31 min (6:56 p.m. to 12:27 a.m., Friday), 5 hr 56 min (5:20 p.m. to 11:16 p.m., Saturday), 3 hr 28 min (2:15 p.m. to 5:43 p.m., Sunday); Brooke, 4 hr 29 min (6:18 p.m. to 10:47 p.m., Friday), 6 hr 55 min (9:23 a.m. to 4:18 p.m., Saturday), 2 hr 52 min (4:26 p.m. to 7:18 p.m., Sunday).

Check, Please!, p. 43

Clue 1: Jermain was the first child in line. Two pizzas, two gallons of milk, and chips add up to $20.13. The child who spent $20.13 was not third in line. Jermain did not spend $20.13.

Clue 2: Roger was the second child in line. Pizza, milk, two loaves of bread, and chips add up to $15.64. Roger did not spend $15.64.

Clue 3: Three pizzas cost $17.97. The fourth child in line did not spend $17.97. Autumn wasn't the third child in line. She also was not the first or second child in line [1, 2]. She was the fourth or fifth child in line.

Clue 4: Chips, two pizzas, and two gallons of milk add up to $20.13. Monique spent $20.13, so she wasn't the third child in line [1]. Monique wasn't first or second in line [1, 2] either, so she was fourth or fifth in line. Franklin was the third child in line (only one). Milk and soap add up to $8.81, so Jermain spent $8.81.

Clue 5: Monique spent $20.13, so she was the fifth child in line. Autumn was the fourth child in line (only one). Autumn did not spend $17.97 [3]. Two loaves of bread, pizza, milk, laundry soap, and chips adds up to $21.87. Autumn and Franklin didn't spend $21.87. Roger spent $21.87 (only one). Autumn spent $15.64 (only one). Franklin spent $17.97 (only one).

Answers: Autumn, fourth, $15.64; Franklin, third, $17.97; Jermain, first, $8.81; Monique, fifth, $20.13; Roger, second, $21.87.

Amassing My Fortune, pp. 44–45

Totals: $39.96, $45.87, $48.32, $53.65, $47.91.

Clue 1: The child who deposited $39.96 was at the bank at 10 a.m. or 11 a.m., so Marlowe deposited her money at 1 p.m. or 2 p.m. Marlowe did not deposit $39.96.

Clue 2: Sean did not deposit his money at 2 p.m. Sean did not deposit $48.32. Marlowe and the other girl are the only ones who could have deposited $48.32. The girl who deposited $48.32 did not deposit it at 10 a.m. [1].

Clue 3: Kasey did not deposit her money at 10 a.m. She did not deposit $45.87. The child who deposited $45.87 did not do so at 2 p.m. and is a boy. Either Kasey or Marlowe deposited $48.32 [2], so Bart and Justin did not deposit that amount. A boy deposited $45.87 (must be Sean, Justin, or Bart).

Clue 4: Justin did not deposit his money at 10 a.m. Justin did not deposit $53.65, and the child who deposited $53.65 did not do so at 2 p.m. A boy deposited at 2 p.m., so either Justin or Bart deposited at 2 p.m. This means that Marlowe deposited her money at 1 p.m., and the child who deposited $39.96 is the child who deposited money at 10 a.m.

Further Reasoning: The child who deposited at 2 p.m. did not deposit $48.32, $45.87 [3], $39.96 [1], or $53.65 [4]. The child who deposited at 2 p.m. deposited $47.91. The boy who deposited $45.87 had to do so at 11 a.m. Kasey then deposited her money at 12 p.m. [3]. If Kasey deposited directly before Marlowe, but Sean deposited money one hour before one of the girls, then Sean must be the child who deposited $45.87 at 11 a.m. Then, Kasey deposited $48.32 [2]. Justin deposited at 2 p.m. (only one) and Bart deposited at 10 a.m. (only one). Bart deposited $39.96 [1]. Marlowe deposited $53.65 [4] and Justin deposited $47.91 (only one).

Answers: Bart, $39.96, 10 a.m.; Justin, $47.91, 2 p.m.; Kasey, $48.32, 12 p.m.; Marlowe, $53.65, 1 p.m.; Sean, $45.87, 11 a.m.

It's Not a Rectangle Number, pp. 46–47

Matrix Blanks: Square Roots (L to R): $^6/_7$, $^3/_{11}$, .272, .583.
Matrix Blanks: Square Numbers (L to R): $^{36}/_{169}$, $^{49}/_{144}$, .391, .213.

Clue 1: Brittin did not calculate for $^3/_{11}$ or .074, but the student who was assigned to calculate the square of $^3/_{11}$ also found its decimal equivalent to be .074.

Clue 2: The student who was assigned to calculate the square of $^5/_8$ did not find .213 as its decimal equivalent. Gloria did not solve problems with $^5/_8$ or .213 in the problem or answer.

Clue 3: Leiko and Gloria were not assigned to solve for $^7/_{12}$. Gloria did not solve a problem with .074 as its decimal equivalent, so she was not assigned $^3/_{11}$ as her problem [1]. Leiko did not find .074 as the decimal equivalent of his problem, so he was not assigned $^3/_{11}$ as his problem.

Clue 4: Brittin and Phillip did not have problems with .213 or $^6/_7$. The student who solved for $^6/_7$ did not find .213 as its equivalent.

Clue 5: Fred did not solve for $^5/_8$. Fred did find his decimal equivalent to be .340, so .340 isn't the decimal equivalent of $^5/_8$.

Further Reasoning: Leiko found .213 as his decimal equivalent (only one). Leiko did not solve for $^7/_{12}$ or $^3/_{11}$, so .213 isn't the decimal equivalent of $^7/_{12}$ or $^3/_{11}$. It also is not the decimal equivalent of $^5/_8$ [2] or $^6/_7$ [4]. So, .213 is the decimal equivalent of $^6/_{13}$ (only one), and Leiko solved for $^6/_{13}$ and .213. Fred's assigned fraction cannot be $^3/_{11}$, so he's either $^7/_{12}$ or $^6/_7$. Do some conversions to solve the rest of the problem. Square $^7/_{12}$ to find $^{49}/_{144}$, then take its decimal equivalent. Fred was assigned to $^7/_{12}$. Then, Brittin was assigned $^5/_8$, Gloria to $^6/_7$, and Phillip to $^3/_{11}$ (only ones). Phillip's decimal equivalent was .074 [1]. If you convert $^6/_{72}$ or $^{36}/_{49}$ to a decimal, you get .734, so Gloria's decimal equivalent was .734, and Brittin's was .391 (only ones).

Answers: Brittin, $^5/_{82}$ or $^{25}/_{64}$ and .625 or .391; Fred, $^7/_{122}$ or $^{49}/_{144}$ and .583 or .340; Gloria, $^6/_{72}$ or $^{36}/_{49}$ and .857 or .734; Leiko, $^6/_{13}$ or $^{36}/_{169}$ and .462 or .213; Phillip, $^3/_{11}$ or $^9/_{121}$ and .272 and .074.

The Brainy Bunch, p. 48

Matrix Blanks: Number of A's: There are 30 A's total, so 13% = 3.9 (4), 17% = 5.1 (5), 20% = 6, 23% = 6.9 (7), 27% = 8.1 (8).

Clue 1: Gregory got one more A than David, so Gregory did not receive four A's and David did not receive eight A's.

Clue 2: Gregory or Miss Story got six A's (.20 × 30 = 6). Miss Story is not David or Gregory.

Clue 3: Anesha, Ella, and Isanti do not have the last name Hardin. Either David or Gregory has that last name. Polk is the last name of a girl, but not Isanti. Either the child with the last name Hardin or Isanti received four A's and the child with the last name Polk received eight A's.

Clue 4: Either Isanti or Ella received four A's (.13 × 30 = 4). One of these two girls is Miss Polk, but it's not Isanti [3]. Isanti received four A's. Ella's last name is Polk and she received eight A's [3].

Clue 5: Either David or the boy with the last name of Bremer received five A's (.17 × 30 = 5). David's last name isn't Bremer. David's last name is Hardin [3] and Gregory's last name is Bremer (only one).

Clue 6: Either Anesha or the girl with the last name of Fay received seven A's (.23 × 30 = 7). Ella's last name is Polk, so the girl whose last name is Fay must be Isanti. Isanti received four A's [4], so Anesha received seven. Anesha's last name is Story [2].

Further Reasoning: If Anesha Story received seven A's, then Gregory received six A's [2]. David received five A's (only one).

Answers: Anesha Story, seven; David Hardin, five; Ella Polk, eight; Gregory Bremer, six; Isanti Fay, four.

Seven Up, p. 49

Matrix Blanks: Celsius (L to R): 21.1°, 27.2°, 33.3°, 37°.
Matrix Blanks: Fahrenheit (L to R): 75.2°, 87.8°, 95°.

Clue 1: Sally does not like the highest or lowest temperature. Summer doesn't like the two lowest temperatures. Skeeter doesn't like the two highest temperatures.

Clue 2: Sawyer likes 70° F, 75.2° F, 81° F, or 87.8° F. Sheldon likes 92° F, 95° F, or 98.6° F.

Clue 3: The only possible combination is for one of the boys to like 75.2° F (24° C) and one to like 27.2° C (81° F). Sawyer and Skeeter are the only ones to like these temperatures.

Clue 4: The only combination that works is for Summer to like 35° C (or 95° F) and Sandy to like 70° F.

Clue 5: Seaton likes 98.6° F. Sheldon likes 92° F (only one).

Clue 6: Skeeter must be 12 years old, so he's 24° C (75.2° F). Sawyer is 81° F (only one). Sally is 87.8° F (only one).

Answers: Sally, 87.8° F (31° C); Sandy, 70° F (21.1° C); Sawyer, 81° F (27.2° C); Seaton, 98.6° F (37° C); Sheldon, 92° F (33.3° C); Skeeter, 75.2° F (24° C); Summer, 95° F (35° C); Skeeter is 12 years old.

Algebar's Algebra, pp. 50–51

Answers to Problems: n = 1 (3n + 4 = 8n − 1), n = 2 (2n + 3 = 4n − 1), n = 3 (n + 6 = 3n), n = 4 (4n − 8 = 2n), n = 5 (3n − 6 = n + 4).

Clue 1: Samantha's partner was not Dixie or Thea. Samantha did not solve for n = 2 or n = 1. Bancroft's partner was not Dixie or Thea. Bancroft did not get n = 5, n = 2, or n = 1 as his answer. Dixie did not get n = 2 or n = 1 as her answer. Dixie's partner is a girl, so she must be partnered with Blythe or Ainsley. Thea did not get n = 1 as her answer.

Clue 2: Bancroft and Heath both did not solve for n = 3. Therefore, Bancroft solved for n = 4 (only one). Bancroft's partner is not Heath. Heath, Dixie, and Thea did not work with Bancroft, so they could not have solved for n = 4. Samantha did not solve for n = 5. Samantha solved for n = 3 (only one). Samantha's partner cannot be Heath.

Clue 3: Blythe and Heath were partners. They did not solve for n = 5.

Clue 4: Misty's partner is a boy, so it must be Bancroft or Troy. She and her partner found n = 4, so Misty must be partnered with Bancroft. Therefore, Samantha's partner was Brad (only one) and they solved for n = 3 [2].

Clue 5: Samantha did not work with Thea. Thea worked with Troy (only one). Thea and Troy solved for n = 2 (only one). Heath and Blythe solved for n = 1 (only one) and Dixie and Ainsley solved for n = 5.

Answers: Ainsley, Dixie, 5; Bancroft, Misty, 4; Blythe, Heath, 1; Samantha, Brad, 3; Troy, Thea, 2.

Coin Club, pp. 52–53

Total Cents Chart: Pennies: Yes on all; Nickels. Yes on 2,365, 2,590, 2,600, and 2,875; No on 2,498. Dimes: Yes on 2,590 and 2,600; No on 2,365, 2,498, and 2,875. Quarters: Yes on 2,600 and 2,875; No on 2,365, 2,498, and 2,590. Fifty cent pieces: Yes on 2,600; No on 2,365, 2,498, 2,590, and 2,875. By elimination, you can find that fifty-cent pieces totaled 2,600; quarters totaled 2,875; dimes totaled 2,590; nickels totaled 2,365, and pennies totaled 2,498.

Clue 1: Quinton's last name is not Penne, and he does not have quarters [Intro.], pennies, or fifty-cent pieces. Penne (boy) isn't the last name of Polly or Fedara. The child with the last name of Penne does not have pennies or fifty-cent pieces.

Clue 2: Polly does not have pennies [Intro.], nickels, or fifty-cent pieces. Penny's last name isn't Nichols. Nichols is the last name of a girl, so Fedara's last name is Nichols. Fedara Nichols doesn't have fifty-cent pieces or nickels [Intro]. Ned, Quinton, and Polly (girl) are not Mr. Quartez. Drew is Mr. Quartez (only one). Drew Quartez does not have quarters or dimes [Intro.].

Clue 3: The boy with the last name of Dimus has either nickels or quarters. The child with the last name of Feeftee has either nickels or dimes. Polly's last name is Feeftee (girl, only one).

Further Reasoning: Ned's last name is Penne (only one), so Ned Penne doesn't have nickels or pennies. Ned Penne also does not have fifty-cent pieces [1]. Drew Quartez has fifty-cent pieces (only one). Quinton has nickels (only one). Quinton's last name is Dimus (only one). Polly Feeftee doesn't have nickels, so she has dimes. Fedara Nichols has pennies and Ned Penne has quarters (only ones).

Answers: Polly Feeftee, dimes; Ned Penne, quarters; Drew Quartez, fifty-cent pieces; Quinton Dimus, nickels; Fedara Nichols, pennies.

The Calendar Kids, p. 54

Clue 1: June's last name is not Weekes. August and March do not have the last name Weekes [boys, Intro.]. Miss Weekes turned in 112,500 tabs. June turned in .96 (4% less) × 112,500, or 108,000 tabs.

Clue 2: Dayton is the last name of a boy, so it is not April, January, June, or May's last name. Dayton didn't turn in 108,000 [June] or 109,125 tabs, because he turned in more than January. January didn't turn in 114,750 (most) tabs, so January turned in 109,125; 111,240; 112,500; or 113,490 tabs. Calculate 102% (2% more) of those, to find the following: 1.02 × 109,125 = 111,307.5 (not a choice), 1.02 × 111,240 = 113,464.8 (not a choice), 1.02 × 112,500 = 114,750 (could be), 1.02 × 113,490 = 115,759 (not a choice). January turned in 112,500 tabs, and the child with the last name of Dayton turned in 114,750 tabs. Dayton is a boy, so only August or March could have turned in 114,750 tabs. The child who turned in 112,500 has the last name of Weekes, so January's last name is Weekes [1].

Clue 3: Calculate 97% (3% fewer) or .97 × 112,500 = 109,125. Miss Yearling collected 109,125 tabs. Miss Dailey collected fewer than Miss Yearling, so she collected 108,000. June is Miss Dailey [1].

Clue 4: Calculate 103% of 108,000 (3% more than June) or 1.03 × 108,000 = 111,240. August had 111,240 tabs.

Clue 5: The boy with the last name Dayviss isn't March, so it's August. March's last name is Dayton. March Dayton turned in 114,750 tabs [2]. May turned in fewer tabs than August Dayviss (111,240), so she turned in 109,125. April turned in 113,490 (only one). Yearling turned in 109,125, so May's last name is Yearling. Munthley is April's last name (only one).

Answers: April Munthley, 113,490; August Dayviss, 111,240; January Weekes, 112,500; June Dailey, 108,000; March Dayton, 114,750; May Yearling, 109,125.

Fill It Up!, p. 55

Matrix Blanks: Miles (L to R): 180 mi., 437 mi., 330 mi., 384 mi., 468 mi., 351 mi., 434 mi.

Matrix Blanks: Gallons (L to R): 12 gal., 23 gal., 15 gal., 16 gal., 18 gal., 13 gal., 14 gal.

Clue 1: The Gadillac did not get 27 mpg.

Clue 2: The Doyota and the Folkswagen did not get 22 mpg. Neither car drove 351 miles.

Clue 3: The 31 mpg trip was a total of 434 miles. Calculate to find that family used 14 gallons of gas. The Shevvy and the Todge did not get 31 mpg.

Clue 4: Calculate the mpg for the Hercedes: 180 divided by 12 equals 15. The Hercedes got 15 mpg.

Clue 5: Calculate the mpg for the first two to fill in blanks on the matrix: 468 divided by 18 equals 26 mpg and 437 divided by 23 equals 19 mpg. Neither the Shevvy nor the Bontiac got 26 mpg or 19 mpg.

Clue 6: Multiply 24 mpg times 16 gallons to find that the total mileage for the car that got 24 mpg was 384 miles. The Todge drove 384 miles [3], so it got 24 mpg and used 16 gallons of gas. The red car is the Gadillac. It got 22 mpg, and it used 15 gallons [1], so you can fill in the matrix blank to note that went 330 total miles.

Further Reasoning: The Shevvy got 27 mpg (only one). The Shevvy did not use 15, 12, 18, 23, 14, or 16 gallons of gas. It did not go 434 miles, 384 miles, 180 miles, 468 miles, 437 miles, or 330 miles. Clue 2 mentions 351 miles. The Shevvy has to be the car that went 351 miles. Divide 351 by 27 to find that the Shevvy used 13 gallons of gas. The Bontiac got 31 mpg (only one). It also used 14 gallons of gas, so you can fill in the matrix blank to note that it went 434 total miles. The blue car is the Folkswagen [2]. The blue car used 23 gallons of gas [6]. The car that used 23 gallons of gas went 437 total miles. Divide 437 by 23 to find that the blue Folkswagen got 19 mpg. That means the Doyota got 26 mpg (only one). The Doyota also has to be the car that drove 468 miles and used 18 gallons of gas [5].

Answers: Bontiac, 31 mpg (434 mi., 14 gal.); Doyota, 26 mpg (468 mi., 18 gal.); Folkswagen, 19 mpg (437 mi., 23 gal.); Gadillac, 22 mpg (330 mi., 15 gal.); Hercedes, 15 mpg (180 mi., 12 gal.); Shevy, 27 mpg (351 mi., 13 gal.); Todge, 24 mpg (384 mi., 16 gal.).

PARdon Moi, pp. 56–57

Tally Chart: Carroll, three pars, two bogies, two double bogies, two triple bogies; Jeane, two birdies, three pars, one bogie, two double bogies, one triple bogie; Jeramie, three pars, four bogies, two double bogies; Paul, one birdie, three pars, two bogies, three double bogies; Sarah, three pars, three double bogies, three triple bogies

Clue 1: Sarah made par on three holes from holes 2, 4, 6, and 8. Carroll and Paul made par on three holes from holes 1, 3, 5, 7, and 9. No one made par on holes 1 and 8, so Sarah made par on holes 2, 4, and 6. That also means that Carroll and Paul's pars came on holes 3, 5, 7, or 9. Paul's scorecard is already filled with a double bogie on hole 5. Therefore, Paul's pars came on holes 3, 7, and 9. Carroll's scorecard is already filled with a double bogie on hole 7, so he made par on holes 3, 5, and 9.

Clue 2: Fill in the tally card with Jeane's tally totals as listed in the clue. She had double bogies on holes 5 and 8, and a triple bogie on hole 7.

Clue 3: Jeramie must have made par on holes 5, 6, and 7. Looking at what is already filled in the on the scorecard, this is the only possible consecutive combination [1]. You can fill in the tally chart to reflect his four bogies and two double bogies. His two double bogies have already been filled in on the scorecard, so his four bogies were on holes 1, 3, 8, and 9. His total score was 43.

Clue 4: Fill in the tally to note that Paul had two bogies, three double bogies, and a birdie. Fill in the scorecard to note Paul's birdie on hole 1. The only shots not filled in on Paul's scorecard are his two bogies. These must have occurred on holes 4 and 8. Paul's total was 42.

Clue 5: One golfer had three triple bogies and another had two triple bogies. Looking at the tally chart, these two golfers could not be Jeane, Jeramie, or Paul. Carroll or Sarah are the golfers with three triple bogies and two triple bogies. The golfer with two triple bogies made those scores on holes 4 and 8. Sarah made par on hole 4 [1]. Therefore, Sarah must be the golfer who made three triple bogies and Carroll is the one who made two. Fill in the scorecard to show that Sarah made triple bogies on holes 1, 5, and 8, and that Carroll made triple bogies on holes 4 and 8. Sarah's scorecard is now completely filled in. Her total score was 50. Another golfer made birdies on the par 5 holes. The only golfer who made multiple birdies was Jeane. Therefore, fill in the scorecard to note that Jeane made birdies on holes 1 and 6.

Further Reasoning: Jeane made par on hole 2 (only one). Add totals on the card to find that Jeane's total score was 41. The only golfer we don't know the total score for is Carroll. One golfer made 47 total points [1]. That must be Carroll. If you add up his totals for the other holes, you find that he made 4 points on hole 3.

Answers: Carroll, 7, 4, 4, 7, 3, 6, 5, 7, 4 = 47; Jeane, 4, 3, 5, 4, 5, 4, 6, 6, 4 = 41; Jeramie 6, 5, 5, 6, 3, 5, 5, 5 = 43; Paul, 4, 5, 4, 5, 5, 7, 3, 5, 4 = 42; Sarah, 8, 3, 6, 4, 6, 5, 5, 7, 6 = 50; Jeane won this game.

Time for Chapter 12, p. 58

Matrix Blanks: Answers: $n = 4$, $n = 5$, $n = 7$, $n = 8$, $n = 10$.

Clue 1: Mady will not teach on Friday. The problem's answer is $n = 5$. The problem taught on Monday does not have the answer of $n = 5$. Mady did not teach the problem with the answer of $n = 5$.

Clue 2: A girl taught on Friday. Neither Pierce nor Ross nor Mady [1] taught on Friday. The problem's answer is $n = 7$. Pierce and Ross did not teach the problem with the answer $n = 7$.

Clue 3: The problem's answer is $n = 4$; this problem will not be taught on Friday. Pierce did not teach on Monday, and he did not teach the problem with $n = 4$ as the answer. Pierce did not teach on Friday [2], so the problem with $n = 4$ as the answer wasn't taught on Thursday.

Clue 4: Ross had to have taught on Thursday or Friday, but none of the boys taught on Friday [2], so Ross taught on Thursday. The problem's answer is $n = 10$. This problem was taught on Monday. A girl taught this problem, so Ross and Pierce did not teach this problem.

Clue 5: The answer to the problem is n = 8. Taleen did not teach this problem. Taleen did not teach on Monday or Tuesday.

Further Reasoning: Mady did not teach on Thursday, so the problem with n = 5 as its answer was not taught on Friday [1]. Pierce did not teach on Thursday, so the problem with n = 4 as its answer was not taught on Wednesday. Pierce did not teach on Friday [2], so the problem with n = 4 as its answer was not taught on Thursday. Therefore, the problem with n = 4 as its answer was taught on Tuesday. Pierce taught on Wednesday [3]. If Pierce taught on Wednesday, then Taleen taught on Friday (only one). Ross taught the problem with the answer of n = 8 on Thursday. Taleen taught the problem with n = 7 as its answer and Pierce taught the problem with n = 5 as its answer (only ones). Mady taught the problem with n = 4 on Tuesday, and Gabbi taught the problem with n = 10 on Monday.

Answers: Gabbi, n = 10, Monday; Mady, n = 4, Tuesday; Pierce, n = 5, Wednesday; Ross, n = 8, Thursday; Taleen, n = 7, Friday.

See You on the Winner's Stand, p. 59

Clue 1: Evey and Owen placed first, second, third, or fourth. Alli placed third, fourth, or fifth. Jess and Kole placed fourth, fifth, sixth, or seventh.

Clue 2: The girl who made eight items placed third. Chad, Kole, Mory, and Owen did not place third or make eight items. Jess did not place third, so she did not make eight items. Evey or Alli placed third and made eight items. The girl who made four items placed first. Chad, Kole, Mory, and Owen did not place first or make four items. Jess did not place first, so she did not make four items. Alli did not place first, so she did not make four items. Evey made four items and placed first (only one). Alli made eight items and placed third (only one). Owen placed in between Evey and Alli, so he placed second [1].

Clue 3: Mory made nine items and placed sixth. Kole did not make nine items or place eighth, eight items or place seventh, seven items or place sixth, four items or place third, three items or place second, and two items or place first. Kole could have made five items and placed fourth or made six items and placed fifth.

Clue 4: Owen placed second, so he made six items. This means Kole made five items (only one) and placed fourth. Jess did not make one item and place fifth or two items and place sixth. Jess made three items and placed seventh.

Clue 5: Chad placed fifth (three places lower than Owen). He made two items (Owen made six).

Answers: Alli, 8 items, 3rd place; Chad, 2 items, 5th place; Evey, 4 items, 1st place; Jess, 3 items, 7th place; Kole, 5 items, 4th place; Mory, 9 items, 6th place; Owen, 6 items, 2nd place.

Takin' My Load on the Road, pp. 60–61

Matrix Blanks: Percent Delivered (L to R): 73, 64, 58, 39, 22, 15.

Matrix Blanks: Percent Remaining (L to R): 27, 36, 42, 61, 78, 85.

Clue 1: Bubba did not deliver the corn or concrete. He also did not drive the truck that had 27,450 lbs remaining after the first drop or the one with 16,200 lbs remaining. The trucks hauling corn and concrete did not have 16,200 or 27,450 lbs remaining after the first stop.

Clue 2: Deedra and Shanna did not deliver corn or soybeans. They also did not drive the trucks that had 38,250 or 12,150 lbs remaining. The trucks hauling corn and soybeans did not have 38,250 or 12,150 lbs remaining after the first stop. One of the moms (either Deedra or Shanna) drove the gasoline or milk truck.

Clue 3: Wayne did not deliver gasoline or milk (carried in tankers). He did not drive the trucks with 35,100 or 16,200 lbs remaining. The trucks hauling gasoline and milk did not have 35,100 or 16,200 lbs remaining after the first stop.

Clue 4: Howard and Charlie did not haul concrete or steel pipes (carried on flatbeds). Neither father drove the truck with 18,900 lbs remaining. One drove the truck with 12,150 lbs remaining and one drove the truck with 16,200 lbs remaining. The trucks hauling concrete and steel aren't the ones with 12,150; 16,200; or 18,900 lbs remaining.

Clue 5: Deedra and Howard did not haul milk or steel pipes. They did not drive the trucks with 16,200 or 18,900 lbs remaining. Howard drove the truck with 12,150 lbs remaining (only one), and Charlie drove the truck with 16,200 lbs remaining (only one). The truck with 12,150 lbs remaining must be hauling gas or milk, but Howard didn't haul milk, so Howard drove the gas truck that had 12,150 lbs remaining.

Further Reasoning: Charlie hauled soybeans and Wayne hauled corn (only ones). The corn wasn't hauled in the truck with 38,250 lbs remaining, so Wayne didn't drive this truck. Bubba drove that truck (only one). Bubba didn't haul concrete [1], so the truck with 38,250 lbs remaining didn't contain concrete. Concrete was on the truck with 35,100 lbs remaining after its stop (only one). Wayne drove the corn truck that had 18,900 lbs remaining after its stop (only one). Deedra drove the truck that hauled concrete and had 35,100 lbs remaining (only one). Shanna drove the truck with 27,450 lbs remaining (only one). One of the mothers drove a tanker of milk, and it wasn't Deedra [5], so it must be Shanna. Bubba hauled the steel pipes (only one).

Answers: Bubba, steel pipes, 38,250; Charlie, soybeans, 16,200; Deedra, concrete, 35,100; Howard, gasoline, 12,150; Shanna, milk, 27,450; Wayne, corn, 18,900.

A Dozen Cousins, p. 62

Matrix Blanks: Missing Amounts (L to R): $2,992; $3,298; $3,408; $3,959; $4,482; $4,704.

Clue 1: Brant, Coot, and Jay are the only ones who raised $3,400; $3,700; and $4,150. They did not raise $3,550; $3,880; or $3,920. Lark, Robin, and Wren are the only ones who raised $3,550; $3,880; and $3,920. They did not raise $3,400; $3,700; or $4,150.

Clue 2: You know that Lark raised either $3,550; $3,880; or $3,920 [1]. Do the calculations to see which possibility would work for Teal's total. If Lark raised $3,550, Teal raised $3,408 (4% less or .96 × 3,550 = 3,408). If Lark raised $3,880, Teal raised $3,724.80 (not an option, because the amounts did not contain cents). If Lark raised $3,920, Teal raised $3,763.20 (not an option), so Lark raised $3,550 and Teal raised $3,408. Robin raised 15% more than Finch. If Lark raised $3,550, then Robin raised either $3,880 or $3,920. If Robin raised $3,880, then Finch raised $3,298 (15% less or .85 × 3,880). If Robin raised $3,920, then Finch raised $3,332. We cannot eliminate either of these, and Finch and Robin's amounts cannot be determined at this point. Jay raised either $3,400; $3,700; or $4,150. If Jay raised $3,400, then Martin raised $2,992 (12% less or .88 × 3,400). If Jay raised $3,700, then Martin raised $3,256. If Jay raised $4,150, then Martin raised $3,652 (not an option).

Clue 3: Wren raised either $3,880 or $3,920. If Wren raised $3,880, Thrush raised $4,656 (20% more or 1.2 × 3,880). If Wren raised $3,920, Thrush raised $4,704. Thrush's total must be somewhere in the two missing amounts at the highest end of the matrix. Brant raised either $3,400; $3,700; or $4,150. If Brant raised $3,400, Mallard raised $3,672 (8% more or 1.08 × 3,400). This is not an option. If Brant raised $3,700, Mallard raised $3,996. If Brant raised $4,150, Mallard raised $4,482. If Coot raised $3,400, Jaeger raised $3,638 (7% more or 1.07 × 3,400). This is not an option. If Coot raised $3,700, Jaeger raised $3,959. If Coot raised $4,150, Jaeger raised $4,440.50, which is not an option. Coot raised $3,700, and Jaeger raised $3,959. Brant raised $4,150 (only one), so Mallard raised $4,482.

Clue 4: Robin did not raise $4,150 [1], so he raised $3,880.

Further Reasoning: Jay raised $3,400 (only one), so Martin raised $2,992. Robin raised $3,880, so Finch raised $3,298 [2]. Wren raised $3,920 (only one), so Thrush raised $4,704 [3].

Answers: Brant, $4,150; Coot, $3,700; Finch, $3,298; Jaeger, $3,959; Jay, $3,400; Lark, $3,550; Mallard, $4,482; Martin, $2,992; Robin, $3,880; Teal, $3,408; Thrush, $4,704; Wren, $3,920. The boys raised a total of $45,443, so they had enough money to build the aviary.

I'm Being Paged—Part I, p. 63

Matrix Blanks: Pages (L to R): 220, 198, 176, 165.

Clue 1: Lewsinda and Janelle did not read the book with 198 pages.

Clue 2: If the book has ⅜ fewer pages, that is the same as having ⅝ of the Ashley's pages (264), which is 165 pages. The books about soccer and wallabies did not have 165 pages.

Clue 3: The soccer book did not have 176 pages.

Clue 4: Brennan's book was about the wallaby. It had either 176 or 220 pages.

Clue 5: Lewsinda did not read about deer, but Janelle read about soccer. Lewsinda must have read about the circus and Stan about the deer (only ones).

Further Reasoning: Stan's deer book had 198 pages (only one). Janelle's soccer book had 220 pages (only one). Lewsinda's circus book had 165 pages (only one). Brennan's wallaby book had 176 pages (only ones).

Answers: Brennan, wallaby, 176 pages; Janelle, soccer, 220 pages; Lewsinda, circus, 165 pages; Stan, deer, 198 pages.

I'm Being Paged—Part II, pp. 64–65

Matrix Blanks: Total Distances (L to R): 203.2 feet, 266.4 feet, 293.6 feet, 305.1 feet.

Clue 1: This clue relates to the students from Part I. Use the chart to record their information. Lewsinda read the circus book (Part I), so she started at the slide. Janelle read the book

that was 220 pages, so she walked a total of 266.4 feet. Brennan began at the swing set. Stan is the child who found his book at the WWI Veterans' bench.

Clue 2: Bert wrote directions for 293.6 feet. Brennan is the child with the book with 176 pages. So, Bert wrote directions starting from the swing set [1], and Brennan traveled a total of 293.6 feet.

Clue 3: The child who started at the fountain walked a total distance of 266.4 feet to the base of Lookout Tower. Janelle walked 266.4 feet, so she started at the fountain and ended at Lookout Tower.

Clue 4: Fujita hid Lewsinda's book. Lewsinda started at the slide [1], so that's where Fujita's directions began. Lewsinda walked a total of 203.2 feet, and Fujita's directions totaled 203.2 feet. Stan started at the pool (only one).

Clue 5: Caela did not make directions for 266.4 feet. She wrote directions for 305.1 feet (only one). She did not hide the book at the mini-golf course. She hid the book at either the WWI bench or the shelter house. Caela's directions started at the pool (only one), so she had to have written her directions for Stan [4]. Therefore, Caela hid Stan's book at the WWI bench, and Stan walked at total of 305.1 feet.

Further Reasoning: Brennan's book was hidden at the mini-golf course (only one), and Lewsinda's book was hidden at the shelter house (only one). Raman hid Janelle's book (only one).

Answers, Books Hidden: Bert, swing set, 293.6 feet; Caela, pool, 305.1 feet; Fujita, slide, 203.2 feet; Raman, fountain, 266.4 feet.

Answers, Books Found: Brennan, swing set, 293.6 feet, mini-golf course; Janelle, fountain, 266.4 feet, Lookout Tower; Lewsinda, slide, 203.2 feet, shelter house; Stan, pool, 305.1 feet, WWI Veterans' bench.

Pop 'N Zip, p. 66

Clue 1: The town with the population of 411 in 1990 had a population of 432 in 2000. Parker's population went from 4,298 to 4,623. Dale and Marcus could not be 411 and 432. Neither city could have 7,870 as its 2000 population.

Clue 2: First, you can eliminate 411 and 432 as the populations of the cities of Craig and Scott. They both increased by more than 21. This means that Floyd had populations of 411 and 432 (only ones). Now, try some calculations. Triple the remaining 1990 populations and add 1,153 to find the possible answers for Scott's populations: 527 × 3 = 1,581 + 1,153 = 2,734 (not an option); 1,206 × 3 = 3,618 + 1,153 = 4,771 (not an option); 1,906 × 3 = 5,718 + 1,153 = 6,871 (not an option); and 2,239 × 3 = 6,717 + 1,153 = 7,870 (is an option). Therefore, Scott's population was 2,239 in 1990 and 7,870 in 2000. Now, double the remaining 1990 populations and add 343 to determine Craig's population: 527 × 2 = 1,054 + 343 = 1,397 (is an option); 1,206 × 2 = 2,412 + 343 = 2,755 (not an option); and 1,906 × 2 = 3,812 + 343 = 4,155 (not an option). Therefore, Craig's population was 527 in 1990 and 1,397 in 2000.

Clue 3: Floyd and Scott do not have 99921 as their zip code. Marcus and Craig do not have 32404 as their zip code. Marcus has a 2000 population of either 1,139 or 1,503. Use these numbers to calculate for its zip code: 1,139 × 44.807 = 51,035 (is an option); and 1,503 × 44.807 = 67,345 (not an option). Marcus' zip code must be 51035 and its 2000 population must be 1,139. Dale's 2000 population must be 1,503 (only one).

Clue 4: Dale's 1990 population is either 1,206 or 1,906. The only possible combination is for its zip code to be 19504. Therefore, its 1990 population was 1,906, and Marcus's 1990 population was 1,206.

Clue 5: Floyd's zip code must be 24091. Scott's zip code must be 70583.

Further Reasoning: Parker's zip code must be 32404. That leaves 99921 as Craig's zip code.

Answers: Craig, 527, 1,397, 99921; Dale, 1,906, 1,503, 19504; Floyd, 411, 432, 24091; Marcus, 1,206, 1,139, 51035; Parker, 4,298, 4,623, 32404; Scott, 2,239, 7,870, 70583.

About the Author

Marilynn L. Rapp Buxton currently teaches in the fourth-, fifth-, and sixth-grade talented and gifted program at Waverly-Shell Rock Community Schools in Waverly and Shell Rock, IA. She also teaches a self-designed curriculum of creative and critical thinking skills in classrooms, is the elementary school yearbook editor, and coaches Future Problem Solving teams. She received a bachelor's degree from Iowa State University and has taken graduate coursework through Drake University, University of Northern Iowa, University of Iowa, Marycrest College, and Viterbo University for her K–12 gifted endorsement and educational certifications.

Her curriculum ideas and student projects have been published as a "Teacher Feature" in *Iowa Talented and Gifted Magazine.* She has enjoyed presenting at the Iowa Talented and Gifted Conference, Midwest Regional Middle Level Conference, area gifted and talented forums, and local staff in-services. She enjoys spending time with family, swimming, participating in choirs, and doing sudoku and matrix logic puzzles.

Common Core State Standards Alignment

Grade	Common Core State Standards in Math
Grade 4	4.OA.A Use the four operations with whole numbers to solve problems.
	4.OA.C Generate and analyze patterns.
	4.NBT.A Generalize place value understanding for multi-digit whole numbers.
	4.NBT.B Use place value understanding and properties of operations to perform multi-digit arithmetic.
	4.NF.A Extend understanding of fraction equivalence and ordering.
	4.NF.B Build fractions from unit fractions.
	4.NF.C Understand decimal notation for fractions, and compare decimal fractions.
	4.MD.A Solve problems involving measurement and conversion of measurements.
	4.MD.C Geometric measurement: understand concepts of angle and measure angles.
Grade 5	5.OA.A Write and interpret numerical expressions.
	5.OA.B Analyze patterns and relationships.
	5.NBT.A Understand the place value system.
	5.NBT.B Perform operations with multi-digit whole numbers and with decimals to hundredths.
	5.NF.B Apply and extend previous understandings of multiplication and division.
	5.MD.A Convert like measurement units within a given measurement system.
Grade 6	6.RP.A Understand ratio concepts and use ratio reasoning to solve problems.
	6.NS.B Compute fluently with multi-digit numbers and find common factors and multiples.
	6.NS.C Apply and extend previous understandings of numbers to the system of rational numbers.
	6.EE.A Apply and extend previous understandings of arithmetic to algebraic expressions.
	6.EE.B Reason about and solve one-variable equations and inequalities.
	6.G.A Solve real-world and mathematical problems involving area, surface area, and volume.
Grade 7	7.RP.A Analyze proportional relationships and use them to solve real-world and mathematical problems.
	7.NS.A Apply and extend previous understandings of operations with fractions.
	7.EE.A Use properties of operations to generate equivalent expressions.
	7.SP.C Investigate chance processes and develop, use, and evaluate probability models.
	7.G.B Solve real-life and mathematical problems involving angle measure, area, surface area, and volume.
Grade 8	8.NS.A Know that there are numbers that are not rational, and approximate them by rational numbers.
Key—Mathematics: CC = Counting & Cardinality; MD = Measurement & Data; G = Geometry; NF = Numbers & Operations—Fractions	

Printed in the United States
by Baker & Taylor Publisher Services